Thomas Paine

In Search of the Common Good

Thomas Paine (1737 – 1809), oil painting by Auguste Millière (1880), after an engraving by William Sharp, after a portrait by George Romney (1792). *National Portrait Gallery*, London.

THOMAS PAINE
IN SEARCH OF THE COMMON GOOD

Proceedings of a colloquium held at the
United Nations in New York
On December 10, 1987,
In celebration of the life and work of

THOMAS PAINE
The 250th Anniversary of His Birth
1737-1987

Published for the first time in observance of the
Paine Bicentennial
The 200th Anniversary of Thomas Paine's Death
1809-2009

EDITED BY JOYCE CHUMBLEY AND LEO ZONNEVELD

SPOKESMAN BOOKS

© United Teilhard Trust, The Netherlands 2009

Rights and permissions to publish individual authors' work and for the reproduction of documents related to the event have been obtained from United Teilhard Trust, the organizers of the UN/UFP/UTT Colloquium on Thomas Paine at United Nations, New York.

Cover Design: Oscar Morera, University for Peace, Costa Rica

First published in 2009 by Spokesman Books
in association with the University for Peace

Spokesman Books
Russell House, Bulwell Lane
Nottingham NG6 0BT
England
Phone: +44 115 9708318   Fax: +44 115 9420433
e-mail: elfeuro@compuserve.com
www.spokesmanbooks.com

Preferred citation:
Chumbley, Joyce and Leo Zonneveld (eds.) (2009)
Thomas Paine: In Search of the Common Good
Proceedings of a colloquium held at the United Nations in New York in celebration of the life and work of Thomas Paine. Published in observance of the Paine Bicentennial. The 200th Anniversary of Thomas Paine's Death 1809-2009. Nottingham, England, Spokesman Books in association with the University for Peace, Ciudad Colon, C.R.

All rights reserved. Permission to make digital or hard copies or portions of this work for classroom use is granted without fee provided that copies are not made or distributed for profit or commercial advantage and that copies bear this notice and the full preferred citation mentioned above. In all other situations, no part of this publication may be reproduced, stored in a retrieval system or transmitted in any form or by any means, electronic, mechanical, photocopying, recording or otherwise, without the prior permission of the publishers.

ISBN 13 978 085 124 762 5

A CIP Catalogue is available from the British Library

Printed by the Russell Press Ltd., (phone +44 115 9784505)

Acknowledgement

For making it possible to bring the history and collective memory on British-born publicist and political renewer Thomas Paine to life at the place he hoped once to exist – humanity's first planetary organization, the United Nations – we thankfully acknowledge the generosity of

ELINORE AND JACQUES DETIGER

International civil servants, academics and specialists whose names, talks and presentations are assembled in *Thomas Paine: In Search of the Common Good,* deserve our gratitude for their wonderful work of seeking and presenting ways towards the establishment of new channels, to address new routes in political communication, and to discover new human realities inspired by Thomas Paine.

THOMAS PAINE FRIENDS, INC.,

and its members generously supported the set-up and initial print-run of the first 200 copies of this book, thus making it possible to preserve and spread Thomas Paine's vision that inspired those present at the United Nations. Apart from TPF's President Irwin Spiegelman, who took the initiative for having this book, financial support was received from:

Maurice Bisheff	Leo W. Zonneveld
Timothy Nelms	Joyce Chumbley
Sherwood Smith	Frances Chiu
James Tepfer	Edward J. Dodson
Mickey J. Hayward	Howard Ennes
John F. Skibiski	Keyth Mallam
Mary and Dana Snyder	Stan Rosenberg
Martha Spiegelman	Kenneth T. Tellis
Robert N. Walsh	

Trevor and Gill Griffiths, both known for their in-depth knowledge of Thomas Paine's work, expressed in exquisite writings and theatrical performances, recommended the editors' manuscript to Spokesman Books. Tony Simpson and Abi Rhodes of Spokesman performed a miracle in getting this handsome book produced in time for Thomas Paine's birthday, celebrated worldwide on 29 January.

We have it in our power to begin the world over again…
The birthday of a new world is at hand.

THOMAS PAINE
Common Sense
(Appendix, 2nd Edition, February 14, 1776)

Foreword

by Joyce Chumbley

A remarkable group of Thomas Paine enthusiasts met at United Nations Headquarters in 1987 on December 10, fittingly, International Human Rights Day, for a colloquium. The panelists comprised a fascinating assortment of individuals: scholars, political leaders, humanitarians, international leaders, an actor, a museum library director, and historians. They assembled to speak of Thomas Paine as a 'Visionary of World Peace.'

Certainly, many people and institutions deserve credit and thanks for inspiring the event and bringing it to fruition. The Thomas Paine Colloquium was organized by the United Teilhard Trust and was presented under the generous auspices of the United Nations, specifically its Peace Studies Unit, and the University for Peace in Costa Rica. Additional support was provided by the Thomas Paine National Historical Association (TPNHA) of New Rochelle, New York, and the Thomas Paine Society of the United Kingdom.

Without doubt, though, the Colloquium was inspired in great measure by two long-time devoted members of TPNHA, Florence Stapleton and Nat Mills, both now deceased. As part of their Paine activities, Florence and Nat created an informal Thomas Paine Readers Club, wrote a modest newsletter, and became more and more determined to launch an activity that would bring the ideas of Thomas Paine to a wider audience. Florence was very well informed about Paine's life and humanitarian ideals, and she was difficult to resist. In Leo Zonneveld, she found an eager collaborator. As founder and director of the United Teilhard Trust, Leo had organized a colloquium on Pierre Teilhard de Chardin the year before at the UN in New York, and he promptly secured that venue again and the support of UN officials for a similar tribute to Thomas Paine.

When, in 1999, the TPNHA determined to stop producing a newsletter, Florence and Nat, Martha and Irwin Spiegelman, and others decided to take on that responsibility and to pursue other projects of their own, such as lobbying for a Thomas Paine Day in each of the fifty states. Meanwhile, Nat gave the Spiegelmans audiotapes of the UN Thomas Paine Colloquium and a copy of the printed program. In 2001, I became a charter member of this new group, and we formed an official non-profit organization, Thomas Paine Friends, with the following mission: *to encourage people to learn about and from Thomas Paine, his times and philosophy so that they may be inspired to participate in public affairs reflective of the spirit of Paine's life, thought, and ideals.*

For Thomas Paine Friends, which did not even exist in 1987, the Colloquium was unfinished business. Irwin Spiegelman contacted Leo Zonneveld about publishing the proceedings from the event, picking up the torch originally lit by Florence and Nat. Leo graciously endorsed the idea. With Leo's assistance, I offered to transcribe the audiotapes, to finish editing the texts, and to prepare the manuscript for publication.

We bring this book forward, then, as a labor of love from the many people who planned and participated in the Thomas Paine Colloquium and who, now, have had a hand in the publication process – all eager to pay tribute to Thomas Paine, a true visionary of peace for all time.

The publication of this book also helps to mark the 200th Anniversary Year of Paine's death on June 8, 1809.

June 8, 2008

Contents

Introduction to the Thomas Paine UN Colloquium Papers by Leo Zonneveld, President, United Teilhard Trust	11
Message from the Secretary-General of the United Nations, H.E. Javier Pérez de Cuéllar, delivered by the Assistant Secretary-General of the United Nations, Luis María Gómez	17
Greetings and Statement by Tapio Varis, Rector of the University for Peace and Chairman of the Colloquium	18
Welcome by Robin Ludwig, Chief of the Peace Studies Unit of the United Nations Secretariat for Political and Security Council Affairs	19
Introduction to the *Visionaries of World Peace* Series of Colloquia, presented by Leo Zonneveld	19
Official Opening by Rodrigo Carazo, President of the Council of the University for Peace	22

Presentations

Michael Foot	*Thomas Paine and the Democratic Revolution*	23
Ian Dyck	*Thomas Paine: World Citizen in the Age of Nationalism*	32
David Braff	*The Forgotten Founding Father: The Impact of Thomas Paine*	39
Eric Foner	*Thomas Paine and American Radicalism during the American Revolution*	44
Charles Francisco	*Thomas Paine: A Most Un-Common Man*	55
Bernard Vincent	*From Social to International Peace: The Realistic Utopias of Thomas Paine*	64
Clive Phillpot	*In the Footsteps of Thomas Paine*	70
Paul O'Dwyer	*Thomas Paine Never Died*	83
Sean Wilentz	*Paine's Legacy*	89

David Henley	*Thomas Paine: An Emerging Portrait*	96
Robert Muller	*Remarks on the Present State of the World, Inspired by the Philosophy of Thomas Paine*	109
Zofia Libiszowska	*The Reality of the Constitutional Vision of Thomas Paine (paper submitted)*	117
References		123
Photographs taken at the Colloquium		130
Contributors		132
Correspondence		134
Name and Subject Index		137
Visionaries of World Peace Series		144

Introduction

Some days in our lives are so remarkable that they are never forgotten. They recall deep-felt experiences that made lasting imprints on our minds. Experiences of courage, of hope, sometimes mingled with despair, carve paths of strength in us under no matter what personal circumstance, but particularly when recollected in relation to – or perhaps felt in confrontation with – courageous people whose deeds are unforgettable, no matter how far in time their lives run back.

Thomas Paine, brilliant activator and humble participant in the process of pointing out the reality of human brotherhood and true democracy, was a man whose heroic, yet often misunderstood life brings effects of emotional recognition that imprint infinitely on the minds of generations of people. The precariousness of human destiny and the conscious awareness of severe limitations to human progress were central to forcefully expressing his vision at stirring times of extreme political uncertainty in France, Britain, and America. Such uncertainty about the human condition is so much alive today where only scenario and circumstance have changed.

Intellectual and philosophical developments in the Age of Enlightenment, for which paradigmatic philosopher Immanuel Kant is seen as the patriarch, led to critical questioning of traditional institutions, customs, and morals endeavouring to supplant the arbitrary authority of aristocracy and established churches. For Thomas Paine *reason* became not only the primary source of and basis for authority, where his *Common Sense* prepared minds for independence, but also the pillar for his moral and religious life. His *The Age of Reason,* outlining his personal creed in the first pages, was published in spite of the backlash he knew would ensue. His thinking and deist arguments find intellectual roots in the traditions of David Hume, Spinoza, and Voltaire.

In publishing this book we offer the memory and heritage of deep-felt experiences from a group of people who, each in his own way, wished to memorialize and exemplify Thomas Paine's authentic and inspired life, lived optimistically in spite of all the burdensome hardships he had encountered from contemporaries whose peaceful and meaningful future he only wished to guarantee and sustain. His unquestionable spirit of freedom, fed by the social and political primacy of reason, and the belief that human beings could better themselves by using their intelligence and moral righteousness, has proved to be irresistible and continues to stir our imagination and action.

This book not only presents scientific analysis of Thomas Paine's life and work but also highlights personal memories from those influenced by his extraordinary character and frame of mind. Delegates came to the Colloquium by invitation of United Teilhard Trust, my brainchild, assisted by the unforgettable perseverance of Florence Stapleton, to United Nations, New York on 10 December 1987, the day on which the 40th anniversary of the Universal Declaration of Human Rights was celebrated. Observations from their own lives presented at the occasion as well as historical and academic work await your attention in the pages that follow.

Michael Foot introduced a Thomas Paine working behind the screens when he reminded delegates that Ronald Reagan and Mikhail Gorbachev had signed a historic nuclear missiles control agreement in Washington, DC two days before this Colloquium. Gorbachev's book on *Perestrojka* – just out and read on his flight to New York – was worth reading he argued, adding that Thomas Paine had anticipated and forecast the whole democratic revolution of the 19th and 20th centuries. The new openness in the former Soviet Union, the Polish elections, and China's movement towards democracy had yet to come two years after Michael Foot spoke. He said that 'no other figure in history – and not merely its virtue – could ever have believed in the power of freedom with Paine's single-minded intensity' and argued that against the forces of censorship and suppression Thomas Paine knew he possessed the implements which could work the miracle: the power of free speech, free writing, and free thought that remain irresistible.

Ian Dyck spoke about Paine as one of the most enlightened cosmopolitans of his day but argues that the idea of world citizenship was not his exclusive monopoly. Radical aspiration to embrace international alliance and world unity had already made its presence in circles at London and Birmingham, he said. A prisoner of Robespierre, erstwhile honorary citizen Thomas Paine was jailed in France until James Monroe secured his release. Ian Dyck mentioned that the global citizen and patriot seemed willing to have 'America or France serve as ideological sponsors for the new world union' but both countries left him reviled and ignored to live out his final years.

David Braff measured Thomas Paine's impact on the American and French Revolutions and explored his defense of the rights of the individual and his trust in the legacy of reason. Braff believes Paine could influence and change the 'course of entire nations to accommodate the needs of the living.' Thomas Paine is described by him as a man of reason who provided the vocabulary and frame of reference for modern political thought. But he also touched upon the personally concerned Paine, who was lending his talents to the cause of individuals in need of his support. Forgotten and vilified founding father Thomas Paine owned a unique personality and possessed the rarest gifts a human being may receive – an original mind.

Eric Foner briefly analyzed *Common Sense* and found that several of the ideas expressed therein were already alive in political circles but never before so forcefully, clearly, and directly expressed as by Thomas Paine. He explained how artisan classes in London and Philadelphia, who were just emerging into political consciousnesses, found deep connectivity with Paine's republican ideology. In accepting progressive perfectibility of humanity, Thomas Paine lifted the concerns of humankind from the parochial to a cosmopolitan level according to Foner. Three key characteristics were responsible for Paine's far-reaching success: his impatience with a past that was characterized by hereditary privilege and patronage politics, acrimonious contempt for institutions that fail to stand the test of reason, and unshakable belief that humans could responsibly shape their own destiny.

Charles Francisco commented on the uniqueness of Thomas Paine as a fearless man who never forgot his roots. He mentioned Paine's uncompromising zeal to edify a new worldview, even if it would cause him to fall from hero to outcast in the face of approaching death. An artist and actor, Francisco recited key passages from many of Thomas Paine's works, interwoven with personal comments, recalling the years after Paine's arrival in the New World until his burial 35 years later. He memorializes the subsequent robbing and transport of his remains in a fine wooden chest, later sold as a piece of furniture and lost forever since.

Bernard Vincent described the road from social to international peace where he found Paine's utopian proposals realistic and clearly ahead of his time. Paine saw world peace as a reward for a 'long, patient and difficult struggle' and developed pacifying ideas to nations through the liberation of trade for maritime commerce. Paine's presentation of the alliance of nations was considered his most original proposal. Bernard Vincent added that Paine had Paul I, Emperor of Russia, in mind as the first President of an Association of Nations where each member, irrespective of its size or the nature of its government, could function as an equal partner in the preparation of peace agreements.

Clive Phillpot brought pictures of historical places depicting Paine's life in Britain to the delegates, shown during his presentation at the Colloquium. His personal journey into the history of America's independence from Britain went through a wealth of books and publications which did make a lasting impression on him. Phillpot's thinking about acquiring US citizenship led him to become interested in Jefferson's role in America's history. The political swing to conservatism, and with it the confrontation with the revival of media-unchallenged and old, reactionary ideas, at his arrival as an alien in the US, severely disenchanted him and very seriously dented his belief in human progress. In Thomas Paine he found the missing essential ideas to reset his compass to progress.

Paul O'Dwyer, American politician and lawyer, said that Thomas Paine's writings had left him with a most disrupted mind, leading him to examine truths previously accepted without question. A public place to attach Paine's name to was one of his goals but interest among city governors appeared minimal. Finally, after a long bureaucratic struggle, Thomas Paine Park was born at his initiative and established in New York across the street from the Prosecutor's office, the Federal Courts, and the Federal Correctional Institution. Paul O'Dwyer mentioned that Tom Paine's name had been invoked at that place by thousands of New Yorkers in defence of an innocent Irishman, six months before the Thomas Paine Colloquium took place.

Sean Wilentz, searching for Thomas Paine's legacy and dearth of official glory through established channels and literature, heralded him as the first of the modern intellectuals, who rejected an obsolete view of the world and urged for a fundamental change in human consciousness. He remarked that Paine touched the experience of three nations: France, Britain, and the USA. Paine never renounced support for the French revolution, not even after his release from prison, taking pride in his association with the Girondin faction. His influential writings were a critical component in the establishment of America's independence. In

England Paine's writings became the foundation texts of the labour movement. Over time, France and the US relinquished their interest in him. Wilentz concluded that Paine's true legacy lives on in the tension between life's unfulfilled visions and the struggle to reform living realities – the source from which his writings still exert their great power to us, today's practical utopians.

David Henley portrayed Thomas Paine by listing all daring and revolutionary initiatives taken by him. To illustrate Paine's remarkable influence on others, he composed two tables with quotes from historians and biographers on the effect of *Common Sense* on American Independence. Henley's third table listed writings supporting the possibility of Paine's authorship of the first draft of the Declaration of Independence. In finishing his series of 'portraits' Henley gave a fascinating account of measures taken by ill-thinking magistrates to avoid or counteract the display of art immortalizing Thomas Paine to the public.

Robert Muller characterized Thomas Paine in staging him as an honest interrogator to political and social leadership in present-day society. In offering critical insights, Paine would never allow public opinion to shape and influence his views; he would question every aspect of societal behaviour and raise issues that should appeal to world government. Muller lets Paine ask penetrating questions about desirable changes at a global level that would reassure the future and destiny of humanity, presenting them one by one as crucial material to institute some of the most wanted social and political revolutions that Paine would likely have recommended if he were here, alive today.

Zofia Libizowska's paper discussed how Paine's political theory translated the political philosophy of the Age of Enlightenment in an ordinary person's vocabulary. Paine demanded immediate proclamation of the Declaration of Independence, which would constitute a document of America's own national sovereignty, built on the principle of the sovereignty of the people and human rights. She pointed out how his vision became instrumental in the composition of America's gift to the world: the first-ever realization of an Agreement by its people. It was embodied by the Continental Charter, an act of the people constituting a government and composed by delegates of each colony immediately after the announcement of independence. Libiszowska described in detail how the document followed Paine's ideas in ensuring that order and righteousness in the new State, to be a federation of republics, were to be effectuated and preserved.

United Nations Secretary-General *Pérez de Cuéllar*'s message to the Colloquium underlined the experience of human brotherhood, held central in Paine's passionate life and thought. Paine believed that true world citizenship could become possible through an alliance of nations, offering new hope for a global future in which individual responsibility, opportunity, and action would interlock to shape one's own destiny.

Thomas Paine's significant contribution to the principle of independence was to provide all stimuli to bring forward a new, just, and modern system of government in which the rights and freedom of all people should be preserved to the benefit of the world and across boundaries of national interests and concerns. Although the complexification of issues has dramatically increased by scientific progress, sociological insights, and pluralism since the times of Milton and Paine, today's requirements are no less utopian: how should it be possible to preserve the cultural domains in which humankind expresses its unique and diversified character, and simultaneously provide a governing structure that ensures maximal responsible freedom to each individual? A rich variety of ideas for political renewal knocks on the door of the established bastion of present-day legitimate representative system of democracy to provide impulses for improvement.

Experts from the domain of the philosophy of science point to John Dewey to discover the connection between people, problems, new objects and environment, or Bruno Latour's hybrid networks between humans and non-humans, alongside the deliberative democracy theory of Jürgen Habermas. Yet there is not in the year 2008 a political statement, testament or will with a validity consistent with humanity's desire to anchor its identity, evolutionary advance, and zest for action at a level congruent with the all-embracing scale of Thomas Paine's visionary eye. That is what makes him an unforgettable example of what it means to be human and to build our future accordingly.

Leo Zonneveld
December 17, 2008

Thomas Paine Colloquium 1987

Message from the Secretary-General of the United Nations, his Excellency Javier Pérez de Cuéllar, to the participants in the Second Colloquium in the series Visionaries of World Peace, celebrating the life and work of Thomas Paine

It is a pleasure to welcome you to the United Nations today for the convening of a colloquium on Thomas Paine, the great Anglo-American political theorist and writer. Your series, *Visionaries of World Peace*, under the auspices of the University for Peace, has my complete support, and I am pleased that this meeting has been organized with the assistance of the Peace Studies Unit of the Secretariat.

The visionary you are honoring today, Thomas Paine, was a courageous man of letters and of action, who gave of himself for the benefit of all humanity. In celebrating his life and work, the University for Peace has chosen a fit subject to exemplify its important task of studying, teaching, and promoting peace.

The University for Peace, having its origins in Costa Rica, reflects the future of a country which, since 1948, has eliminated its armed forces by constitutional means. The fact that a disarmed nation can live in peace and radiate the message of peace throughout the world has been demonstrated most recently by the imaginative efforts of President Óscar Arias, who this year was honored with a Nobel Peace Prize.

Thomas Paine, who was born two hundred and fifty years ago, wrote and lived with a keen sense of urgency. The basic premises of his *Rights of Man* were that there are natural rights, common to all men, and that only democratic institutions are able to guarantee those rights. On this very day next year, we will be celebrating the fortieth anniversary of the Universal Declaration of Human Rights, one of the first major achievements of the United Nations.

Much of Paine's thought is relevant today. Perhaps what is most memorable is the effort he made to point out the reality of human brotherhood, which he envisaged in a great republic of all the nations of the world. Thomas Paine's idea of having an 'Association of Nations' dates back to 1800. On 6 October of that year, the author of *Common Sense* sent a plan to his friend, Thomas Jefferson, who approved it. The

Paine Plan recommended ten peaceful ways for settling disputes, including a boycott of aggressor nations.

I salute this great visionary of world peace, whose passionate search for freedom and brotherhood has greatly contributed to the nobility of humanity. And I sincerely hope that your efforts will enhance the quest for peace in the world today.

Greetings and statement by Tapio Varis,
Rector of the University for Peace and Chairman of the Colloquium

As Rector of the University for Peace, I have been asked to chair the Colloquium on Thomas Paine in the series *Visionaries of World Peace*. It is today that President Óscar Arias Sánchez, President of Costa Rica, is receiving the Nobel Prize for Peace. I have the privilege of living and working in that peaceful, voluntarily disarmed country of Costa Rica. When awarding the Nobel Prize, the Commission brought into the formulation of its wording that the process of peace has importance beyond the region where its impact and activities prove extraordinarily strong.

It is of great importance that we are convening this Colloquium at a time that the leaders of the two super powers, Mr. Ronald Reagan and Mr. Mikhail Gorbachev, are meeting in this country, the United States of America. And it is particularly inspiring to see that the list of speakers for today consists of distinguished scholars, intellectuals, politicians, people who know about peace, who have worked hard for peace. Costa Rica has been keeping a tradition of peace much longer than the media have been focusing specific interest upon its role in Central America. Being a Finnish citizen myself, I have great admiration for former President José Figueres, Don Pepe, who is over eighty years old and is still actively participating in peace-related activities. Former President Rodrigo Carazo, the founder of the University for Peace, is here with us, presiding over the Colloquium.

The people of Costa Rica are deeply desiring peace for the world and are continuing their historically important work in Central America that would be recognized internationally as an important model. May the model of democracy for which Thomas Paine fought help us again in designing the future with inspiring new visions for world peace.

Welcome by Robin Ludwig, Chief of the Peace Studies Unit of the United Nations Secretariat for Political and Security Council Affairs

As Chief of the new Peace Studies Unit, it is really a pleasure for me to welcome you all here. I speak also on behalf of the Under Secretary-General for Political and Security Council Affairs, who knows that you are meeting here today and takes great interest in what you are interested in yourselves.

The Peace Studies Unit actually originated and goes back to the International Year of Peace, which was celebrated in 1986. The Unit was created this past year in response to the support that was expressed by people around the world for the ideals of the Year of Peace. Even though the year ended, the stream of mail and telephone calls kept coming in to the United Nations. The Secretary-General decided someone should be there to answer. So, the Peace Studies Unit was created in order to serve as a clearinghouse for activities related to the promotion of peace, activities by non-governmental organizations, such as the University for Peace, and also organizations in the academic area.

It is our task to collect ideas and assist where we can to help people in promoting peace in various ways. And that is why we feel your meeting today is very important, because although we are deeply involved with aspects of conflict resolution and the work of the Security Council, all of this work goes back to certain basic values and principles. It is important for people to get together and discuss what those values are, what our common ground is, so that we can work further on that basis. I hope this will be a very good meeting.

Introduction to the Visionaries of World Peace Series of Colloquia by Leo Zonneveld, President, United Teilhard Trust

Who is this being called man? What are the expectations for human life; what is the future of the human phenomenon? Questions like these were being asked at the first colloquium in the series, *Visionaries of World Peace*, celebrating the life and work of Pierre Teilhard de Chardin. I think these are valid questions. For we cannot hope to answer the question what peace is, if we do not want to know who man is.

Peace is a state of mind; a healthy, active, and intelligent equilibrium in the mind of man which has its natural reflection in the Global Brain, in the dual role of both activator and participant. Man is a constructor of new dimensions. Humankind's visionary eye feeds the imaginative mind and brings itself to action in thought and deed, satisfying the urge for existential meaning. In order to find existential meaning, there is a need to cooperate, to speak with, to work with others. There cannot be a healthy mind without a synthesis of all that is experienced as known, as true, at the summit of one's personal reality.

This is certainly true for the visionary whose life and work we are celebrating today, the great American writer and political genius of British descent, Thomas Paine. The man, the patriot, whose writings did more for the American cause in the Revolution than did any other single factor, also proposed arbitration and international peace as a humanitarian. Thomas Paine suggested a great republic of all nations of the world, and proposed an international flag for it: the colors of the Rainbow. Here in the building of United Nations, the visionary Paine as a constructor of new dimensions, brilliant activator and humble participant, can not fail to stir our imagination. For Thomas Paine, it is true what Russell Davenport wrote referring to Arthur, the once and only King:

(A)…sword of vision and great pain,
Which Arthur drew, which all man draw,
By some enchantment of the law,
And fling back to the gods again.[1]

The Romance of King Arthur and his Knights of the Round Table also tells us about Galahad, who drew out the sword from the floating stone at Camelot. The enchanting call from the sword in the stone repeats itself time and time again for those who are courageous enough not to ignore it. The meeting between a human being and the impossible is arranged continuously, as the author of *Common Sense* must have felt many times. And those who obey, people like Thomas Paine, may perhaps only become victors in the eyes of God and at the price of great suffering. The life and work of constructors of new and undreamt-of dimensions, visionaries of world peace, men and women such as Thomas Paine, are celebrated, recalled at occasions like these at United Nations Headquarters.

Our organization is called United Teilhard Trust only because it derives its principles, activities, ideas, and vision from the French scientist Teilhard de Chardin, to whom, as I said earlier, we devoted our

first colloquium at the United Nations. Teilhard de Chardin found both his sword in the stone as well as peace by asking himself: can I, 'this quantity of consciousness, which is thrown alive in the thorns,' become the embryonic eye of discovery in the Cosmic Being which is now forming itself in mankind? United Nations Secretary-General Dag Hammarskjöld found peace by asking: can this human body in which I find myself, 'this accidental meeting of possibilities, which calls itself I'[2] ... become a passionate instrument of direction in its Global Brain?
On the first page of Hammarskjöld's diary it is made clear that the stone in front of him did not give up the sword easily; every human undertaking is at some stage an act of faith. Hammarskjöld says:

> I am being driven forward
> Into an unknown land.
> The pass grows steeper,
> The air colder and sharper.
> A wind from my unknown goal
> Stirs the strings
> Of expectation.[3]

Driven forward we are, each of us individually, on a journey of faith – a journey which may bring us to the sword in the stone, a sheer impossible meeting with the unknown and the supreme, the yet unexpressed potential of human endeavor, of human energy. Each of us may find a challenge in trying to draw it out.

I would like to thank my colleagues and friends in New York, New Rochelle, and Escazú, Costa Rica, who worked so hard to make this Colloquium on Thomas Paine happen. It is such a pleasure for me to see many friends around in this conference room from as far afield as France and California: Monsieur Maurice Ernst, who heads the Fondation Teilhard de Chardin and the Brain/Mind specialists Jean Houston and Marilyn Ferguson.

I sincerely hope and pray that the great work of Thomas Paine will be continued, perhaps in a different spectrum of human awareness, for the soul of humankind cries out for sense, for meaning and understanding, again. And I am sure that the Gods have firmly planted the sword in the stone in front of today's speakers as well as before each and every one of us. It will encourage us to act heroically, in the true sense of the heroic spirit, in fulfilling ultimately our destiny as constructors of new dimensions.

Statement and official opening by Rodrigo Carazo, President of the Council, University for Peace

Thomas Paine – his thinking was simple, open, and clear. The accuracy of his words commanded the attention of readers, making them grasp the full breadth of his message with all its contrasts. He thus arose, in the world of his time, a deep concern for, and a commitment to the nation.

He appealed not only to reason but also to human emotions. He sought to encourage the free flow of the imagination, while hoping that each individual could use his or her own intelligence. He was masterful and forceful in the propagation of his ideas.

He was a true believer in Justice. He advocated distribution of wealth from those who have more, to the benefit of the dispossessed, the old, and the needy. With his thinking, he ploughed deeply the seed of the democratic and republican ideals.

The people of the United States of America of that time, with the election of Jefferson, ratified the teachings of the Founding Fathers. Among them, Thomas Paine, who was universal and not parochial, reached outstanding fame in his lifetime and continues to do so today. His fame lived on as a result of his existential quest, which opened the way to a humanitarian, spiritual, and revolutionary attitude. This is at the root of his worldwide call for Justice, and its corollaries, Liberty and Peace.

The University for Peace is honored to open this Colloquium on Thomas Paine. As a visionary of world peace, he will get all our attention and our study. This is the best way for us to pay tribute to the man who left us ideas whose benefits humanity is still harvesting.

Michael Foot

Thomas Paine and the Democratic Revolution

Mr. Chairman and Mr. President, I make one or two brief preliminary words of thanks for those who have organized this Colloquium. I can assure you that we owe a great debt to the United Teilhard Trust and to all those who arranged this meeting. And, speaking on behalf of the Thomas Paine Society in Britain, we would like to express our great good wishes to you for the way it has been arranged and for the thought in arranging it and for the details and kindness we have been shown. And especially, I know all my friends from England would wish me to stress this: Robert Morrell is the real person who sustained the Thomas Paine Society in England. Many of you who have been to England and studied there, or in other ways have met him, know that there is not the slightest doubt that there would not have been a Thomas Paine Society kept alive in England if it had not been for Robert Morrell. He is the person who should really be here making the response, but I would wish to send his good wishes to the Colloquium, too.

As I came across, flying to New York to take part in this occasion, throughout last night, or whenever it was, I have forgotten the exact timetable, but I thought it was a stunning time to come to such a meeting as this in New York, all arranged under the auspices of Thomas Paine, of course. Indeed, it might be said that he had fixed most of the arrangements and that neither of the two chief leading people [President Reagan and General Secretary Gorbachev] who are engaged in ceremonies elsewhere throughout this week would have been able to carry through their operations at all if it had not been for Thomas Paine. I am sure that would have been Thomas Paine's conclusion because he quite often took a very properly elevated view of his own achievements. But even this might have been a bit beyond his comprehension.

But it is perfectly true that if it had not been for Thomas Paine none of us would have been sitting around this table, and if it had not been for Thomas Paine it would not have been possible for this great occasion – because I think it is a great occasion – to have taken place in this Republic over these last two days and for the [nuclear non-proliferation] agreement that has been reached. Of course we are all hoping that it is going to go very much further still. But it is made in the spirit of Thomas Paine. It is made in the spirit of drawing back from the precipice which seemed to be opening before the world, and so it is a momentous week for all of us. Under no better auspices than those of Thomas Paine could we meet to agree to celebrate.

I was also partly prompted in these thoughts because muddled up in my mind with Thomas Paine, whom I was reading as I came across through the night, I was also reading some other people, too – some of the works of the President of this Republic and of the General Secretary of the Soviet Union.

I was reading the latest book by Mikhail Gorbachev, and I recommend everybody to read it. He is not as good a writer as Thomas Paine, I may say, but it is a very good book, nonetheless. I believe that it is a book pretty well every word of which is written by him, and it is very difficult to read that book and not think that it is not the achievement of somebody who really does want to tell the world what he is thinking, what he is doing, and what he hopes to achieve. It is certainly not the book of somebody who is churning out something for purely propaganda purposes. There is one sentence there that struck me. And, again, I am sure it would not have been written if it had not been for the existence of Thomas Paine. For Mikhail Gorbachev writes in his book, describing the atmosphere of what is happening in the Soviet Union: 'Today it is as if we were going through a school of democracy again.' I hope he is. His democracy is not the kind of democracy in which people believe in the United States, or in Britain or France, or in most of the Western world. It is not the same democracy as that which Thomas Paine hoped to bring into being. But, nonetheless, I do believe that it is something different from what went before in the Soviet Union. It is not the kind of democracy which was the tired, debased use of the word which previous operators in the Soviet Union have employed, in my judgment. I believe that there is a school of democracy through which Mr. Gorbachev has been reared. And in the book he describes how hundreds of people in the Soviet Union have been writing to him about what is happening there, or what is not happening there, and of course he is now having the same experience all over the world. I think that is a very important development. Maybe Thomas Paine was watching over Mikhail Gorbachev when he wrote those parts of the book.

As for the President of this Republic, he is also another of Thomas

Paine's pupils. He, maybe, does not always acknowledge it, but it happens to be the case. A few years ago, in 1984 I think it was, I was slightly startled to switch on a television program and I heard President Reagan quoting the words of Thomas Paine. I did not know he was so familiar with the works of our hero or his deeds even, but still he quoted him without any disparagement whatever, and I think we should take these things as we find them. President Reagan said, quoting Thomas Paine, 'We have it in our power to begin the world over again,' one of the great and famous phrases of Thomas Paine that went around the world. As I say, when I heard that speech by President Reagan first, I thought one of his speech writers had done it for a wager. I thought somebody had said: 'I bet you can't get in a quotation from Thomas Paine.' But, you see, Thomas Paine carries through his education in the strangest ways.

Here now, I believe that in this week the world has seen by far and away the most hopeful development since the invention of nuclear weapons, and I believe that it can lead the world along the path to the total abolition of these weapons, and I am sure that Thomas Paine would approve.

Thomas Paine's reputation has grown steadily over recent years. This Colloquium is one sign of his worldwide recognition. The next few years will see a further enlargement of his fame and honor, since the events in which he played a unique role are, most properly, to be commemorated even by those who may never have known his name. Both the land of his birth and the land of his adoption have been seeking to make some amends for the outrages they committed against him during his life. However, it is the French Revolution of 1789, with all its endless political and intellectual reverberations, which now seems more than ever a dominating event in world history. Thomas Paine prepared the way for it by his role in the American Revolution. He became a leading instigator of the English Revolution which was still unborn.

He was the first ardent exponent of *democracy* when that word, in its modern connotation, had scarcely appeared in the dictionary. Yet he always knew what he meant; and he said it in plain English. This last was his most revolutionary act. His English language has become as near to a universal language as the world has ever known. And it is no bad thing for the world that he always strives, and so often succeeds, to speak the language of common sense, human rights, hatred of empires, and –

despite all his natural belligerence – a true love of peace and a new international order.

Now, these few introductory remarks were meant to be very brief. But it is natural for Thomas Paine to take command, and transform his immediate struggle into one of universal significance. That is what he was always doing in every battle in which he was ever engaged. I must not be distracted from mentioning some of the recent or prospective events in the fields of publishing or propaganda which will help to ensure the fresh return of his doctrines and his writings. Penguin Books has published, most appropriately on both sides of the Atlantic, *The Thomas Paine Reader*. And there are some copies available here, thanks to Leo Zonneveld, who has carried them right across New York after considerable labor – all the more to be treasured on that account. Never before have so many of his essential writings been concentrated into one volume. I am not saying that there are not other parts of Paine's writings that are still extremely valuable, but there has been an attempt made to concentrate as many of the very greatest ones in one volume. Only in 1945 in the massive two volume edition edited by Philip Foner, or in 1892, in the six volume edition of Paine's *Life and Writings*, compiled by Moncure Conway, have more of his writings been conveniently collected together.

This year, also, the beginnings of a new major biography by George Spater has been published. He had already written a new modern biography of William Cobbett, which added greatly to the literature of our country in that period, and he was the right man to do the same for Thomas Paine. His death deprives us of that completed work, but the pages already available prove what a treasure it would have been, and indeed the pages themselves now, those which have been gathered together, make an indispensable addition to the Paine library. Meantime, in England our foremost modern philosopher, Sir Alfred Ayer (if I can call him that – I dare say he wouldn't object – and he is the true successor of Bertrand Russell), has chosen Thomas Paine to succeed his recent biography of Voltaire. Meantime also, we should not forget to mention – Thomas Paine would allow no such oversight – that our greatest film producer, Sir Richard Attenborough, who made *Gandhi* and *Cry Freedom*, the film which exposes the infamy of apartheid, has chosen as his next subject, Thomas Paine. I am sure he will do it on the spacious and imaginative scale that is required. Once again, the choice is startlingly appropriate. Thomas Paine was one of the very first exponents of the iniquities of imperialism – of the British variety on the Indian sub-continent or of slavery on this one.

The greatest of great men must be judged by their understanding of the age in which they live and the imprint they leave on those that follow. On this double test, Thomas Paine, was the greatest Englishman of the eighteenth century, when there was no shortage of competitors. He was the man who supplied the link between the three revolutionary movements of the epoch, in America, France, and Britain.

Yet, 'Mr. Common Sense,' as he liked to be called when he first started writing here on this continent, was denounced as a drunkard, a wife-deserter, a traitor, a blasphemer, a most profligate wretch without a single redeeming virtue, in Theodore Roosevelt's notorious phrase, 'a filthy little atheist,' gracelessly changed to deist when he realized he had been wrong about that, too, but still with the emphasis on the filth. From this contrast and catalog, it might be assumed that the story is the familiar one of the prophet without honor in his own country and period who eventually reaps his deserts in the eyes of posterity. But not at all: the history of Thomas Paine and his reputation is a much more topsy-turvy affair, and indeed casts a most bizarre light on the whole twisted process of historical judgment.

For Paine, in his lifetime, commanded a notoriety and popularity such as only pop-stars may have today. He wrote the best political best-seller of all time, second only to the Bible. He was idolized by mobs as well as detested by the kings and courtiers and hangers-on whom he lambasted. He was already acclaimed for his pre-eminence by contemporaries whose fame soon became much more securely established than his own – by George Washington, by Thomas Jefferson, by William Cobbett, by Napoleon, who allegedly said when he unearthed his hero in a Paris garret: 'A statue of gold ought to be erected to you in every city of the universe.' It was from such heights that his name and glory were dragged down into the dirt, and the more one looks back upon the episode, the more one is driven, against the normal probabilities, I would say, to accept the notice of a kind of sinister Establishment conspiracy.

Most of the accusations against his private life are false or misleading or unbalanced. Many of them derived from a posthumous political spite or perhaps rather from the irrepressible fears which he planted in orthodox minds or hardened hearts or comfortable ruling cliques. Not only was Thomas Paine a true revolutionary; he invented for his purposes a plain, downright English style which everyone could understand. He anticipated and forecast the whole democratic revolution of the nineteenth and twentieth centuries, and, in particular, his tone of voice runs through all the great utterances of American freedom, from the Declaration of Independence itself, to the Gettysburg Speech and the finest burst of Franklin Rooseveltian eloquence. The Declaration of Independence – I know that some of the historians have argued about it – but the Declaration of Independence, wrote H. G. Wells with all his English modesty, is 'one of those exemplary documents which it has been the peculiar service of the English to produce for mankind.' And there is something in what he said. Dispute may be possible about Paine's exact role in its drafting; but without Paine's influence, without the method of pamphleteering he had brought with him from London to Philadelphia, could Thomas Jefferson have written in those terms? I think it is extremely difficult to imagine that he could have done, and therefore he played a major part at the critical moments of the foundation of this great Republic.

Nothing could shake his own conviction that within his own lifetime or slightly afterwards – and thanks largely to his own Atlas-like exertions – the world would be turned upside down. He knew he possessed the implement which could work the miracle – the power of free speech, free writing, and free thought. Nothing could induce in him a hairsbreadth of doubt; the bigger the bonfires they made of his books, the bigger would be the sales. No other figure in history can ever have believed in *the power of freedom* – and not merely its virtue – with Paine's single-minded intensity. That was his secret. 'Mankind,' he said, with his grand simplicity, 'are not now to be told that they shall not think, or they shall not read.' And incredibly, he was proved right, as near as mortal man can be.

Time and time again, both in his lifetime and in the years since his death, the forces of censorship and suppression thought they could exterminate him and his ideas forever. Time and again, those forces have been shown that his free word was too strong for them. English courts brought in the verdict of high treason, but they could not stop the sale of the *Rights of Man*. The men in power in Paris would have sent him to the guillotine, but they could not stop his writing *The Age of Reason*.

An American President would have stripped him of his good name as a citizen of the United States of America, he who had been the first almost certainly to frame that famous title, but every succeeding generation of American citizens turned back to his pamphlets which first called upon the American people to declare their independence and to summon their uttermost powers of resistance, in their darkest times. He, more than anyone, took the trouble to explain why the cause of American revolt against English oppression was the cause of all mankind. And the words are still there, still burning on the page. They retain their force today, in Asia, Africa, in the old continent and the new ones.

I do not say these things only to honor a great Englishman who became and boasted that he was a citizen of the world, although that would have been a good enough reason. I say them also because so much of what he said remains startlingly relevant, indeed still revolutionary.

If he were writing today, there is no doubt he would give his blessing to the Agreements that have been signed here on this continent during this week. He would give his blessing to the foundation of the United Nations and its Charter; he would be demanding only that those provisions should be more rigorously and adventurously applied. We were mentioning before that the right of small nations should be remembered during this week. Their rights are enshrined in the Charter of the United Nations more plainly than in any previous document or by other diplomatic means.

If Paine were writing today, he would give the backing of his international vision to the cause of strengthening the United Nations and its Charter. He was one of the very first writers who started to develop the ideal of settling international disputes by arbitration, and not the resort to arms.

If he were writing today he would certainly give his support to arms control. Indeed, I cannot believe that he would not be giving his full support to the pursuit of the abolition of nuclear weapons in their entirety. I recommend some passages in the Gorbachev book, a quite exceptional passage in the writing of a leading political figure throughout the world. Gorbachev describes in that book what happens if great powers try to uphold the logic of saying that they have the right to keep nuclear weapons because that is the only way they could be defended. He argues with many of them – I will not now specify who they are but the British Prime Minister happens to be number one on the list – when they seek to argue that only by nuclear weapons can we protect ourselves. The British Prime Minister has dared to go on television in the Soviet Union and say that nuclear weapons were the only means of enabling the small countries to protect themselves against the large ones, and Mr. Gorbachev had to do his best to dismantle such a lunatic piece of logic. In the book he does it very politely but extremely effectively. So I hope that will be another enticement for people to read the book. I have not the slightest doubt that we are going to be arguing about this for a number of years ahead, but where Thomas Paine would be urging us on to fresh fields of achievement, no doubt about that.

If he were writing today, Thomas Paine would be seeking to create a fresh system for educating the whole of the world in our modern dangers and modern perils, and in the means of escape from them. We have had in Britain over these past ten to fifteen years one of the best developments, in my opinion, that of the Open University, which offers a modern education, by modern means of communication – radio and television – the possibilities of a university education for multitudes of people who would not have been able to consider it before. I have in my own constituency in Wales numbers of people who were thrown out of the pits or the steel works, or lost their jobs in their forties and fifties who previously would have had no chance of thinking how they might have been able to make full use of a university education. Thanks to the Open University, they have been able to do so. I do not think we use this wonderful instrument in anything like the scale that we should, but there it is. Now it is proposed that under the Commonwealth aegis or name, there should be a Commonwealth University, whereby these new means should be used to spread forms of education. I do not advocate the imposition of some centralized doctrine to be spread, but we should use the power to communicate such as we never had at our disposal before. And we must use it for the highest educational purposes. Thomas Paine would approve.

In his last major book, most of which is included in this Penguin reader I have referred to, *Agrarian Justice*, which he wrote just before his return to the American Republic – which, alas, had turned its most severe countenance upon him – he came to a sad and tragic homecoming. In that book, at that moment, he still proclaimed more confidently than ever:

'An army of principles will penetrate where an army of soldiers cannot. It will succeed where diplomatic management would fail. It is neither the Rhine, the Channel, or the Ocean that can arrest its progress. It will march on the horizon of the world and will conquer.'

That is what Thomas Paine believed. He could make a half-sentence sound like a tocsin. He worked the miracle – as his friend William Blake exaggerated – of defeating whole armies with a pamphlet and, more miraculously still, his battle cries retain their force two hundred years later. So, certainly there was something worth celebrating in calling this Colloquium.

Ian Dyck

Thomas Paine: World Citizen in the Age of Nationalism

'My attachment is to all the world, and not to any particular part'
Paine, *Crisis VII*

Thomas Paine was an English citizen by birth; he also became a citizen of the United States and an honorary citizen of France. Although multinational citizenships were not frequently awarded by Western governments during the late eighteenth century, when a nascent nationalism restricted the exchange between nations of persons and ideas, Paine moved freely between England, France, and America, championing the rights of world humanity, and seldom concerning himself with national boundaries or with political traditions.

Most of Paine's supporters in each of his three countries did not share his disregard for national identity. They might have had world ideological sympathies but they felt a peculiar loyalty to their native country. For Paine, however, national citizenships were but so many licenses of physical mobility. He never regarded himself as a citizen of this or that country; he perceived himself as a global patriot, a citizen of the world. If national boundaries there must be, he suggested, let there also be a forum of united nations to advance world peace and the liberty of peoples. A century and a half later such a forum would be erected, but its early prophet would largely be forgotten – a victim of the political reaction and narrow nationalism of the previous two centuries.

Thomas Paine was not the first person to claim world citizenship. Socrates, according to Plutarch, identified himself, not as a Greek or an Athenian, but as a *mundanus* – a world citizen.[4] Although Paine read neither Latin nor Greek, he almost certainly was familiar with the works of Joseph Addison and Viscount Bolingbroke, who in the early eighteenth century laid claim to world citizenship.[5] Stoic philosophy, with its ideological commitment to cosmic or world citizenship,[6] also reached Paine through his friend Oliver Goldsmith, whose *The Traveller* and *Citizen of the World* were in part philosophical critiques of the local attachments of the English. The eighteenth-century English were accepting of international scrutiny of their manners and morals; above all they enjoyed modeling their political institutions before world opinion.

Paine, however, did not wish to model England; it was his native country but not a special haven of liberty and popular rights. He held the same opinion of his countrymen: they were neither freer nor more innately liberal than the nationals of other countries.

The extraordinary absence of instinctive patriotism removed Paine intellectually and emotionally from the great mass of Englishmen. It put him in correspondence with cosmopolitan thinkers such as Goldsmith, and with the great American Benjamin Franklin,[7] whose predilection for world citizenship caught the attention of the young Paine. Although Paine's world citizenship was unique in its purity, Franklin consciously cultivated the personage of the noble savage of the American frontier. Thomas Jefferson, Paine's most loyal ideological ally, revered France and its Revolution, but towards Britain he harbored love-hate sentiment, wishing at times for 'an ocean of fire between that island and us.'[8] Even Samuel Johnson, often cited as the greatest representative of eighteenth-century sensibility, once announced that he was 'willing to love all mankind, except an American.'[9] If even Johnson, for whom patriotism represented 'the last refuge of a scoundrel,' freely indulged in national aspersion, Paine must be regarded as one of the most enlightened cosmopolitans of his day.

The extent of Paine's internationalism was foreshadowed in his earliest writings, although it was partially obscured by his revolutionary rhetoric. In America, his expressed hostility towards the deeds of the British government and monarchy were readily interpreted by the aroused Americans as symptoms of hostility towards all things British, while his personal exhortations to Americans to proclaim their independence, and to be 'patriots' all, were interpreted in terms of territorial and political sovereignty. But in *Common Sense* Paine sharply ridiculed the predilection of individuals to define themselves according to parish, county, or country. People should unite around reason, he declared: 'The prejudice of Englishmen in favor of their own government by king, lords, and commons, arises as much or more from *national pride* than reason.'[10]

Regardless of its ideological guise, national pride was anathema to Paine. He understood a 'patriot' as someone loyal to universal principles of equality and liberty. Hence the American Revolution was not simply about secession from Great Britain, as he announced in *Common Sense*, 'The cause of America is in a great measure the cause of all mankind.'

Or as he put it elsewhere in the same text, 'We have it in our power to begin the world over again.'[11] Paine's meaning in these stirring phrases was lost on even the most world-minded of the American Revolution. Jefferson himself rummaged deep in the history of England for Saxon democratic precedent, while for republican models he pondered the political experiments of the Ancients. Paine alone was entirely comfortable in framing institutions according to universal and 'common sense' principles, without consulting with history or national tradition.

Paine returned to England in 1787, preceded by his reputation as a revolutionary republican. Some English reformers were of the opinion that Paine had betrayed England by his support of the American cause in the Revolutionary War, but others were citizens of the world, fully accepting of the American revolt and the Declaration of Independence. The latter now looked to Paine for ideological leadership in their own campaign for parliamentary reform.[12]

Upon the outbreak of the revolution in France, the radical reform societies in Britain sent messages of congratulation to the National Assembly and later to the Convention, celebrating the demise of tyranny and the prospects of world peace through a world fraternity of citizens devoted to liberty and equality.[13] In its address to the French nation the London Corresponding Society anticipated an alliance 'not of crowns, but of the people of America, France, and Britain.' Even the executive of the London Revolution Society – the most 'respectable' and aristocratic of the English reform associations – offered the French revolutionaries a message of congratulation. Identifying its members as 'Men, Britons, and Citizens of the World'[14] the Society's executive announced its disdain for 'national partialities,' and celebrated the example of France as an encouragement to 'other nations to assert the unalienable rights of mankind, and thereby to introduce a general reformation in the governments of Europe, and to make the world free and happy.'[15]

Similar sentiments abounded in British radical circles. Joseph Priestley, leader of the Constitutional Society in Birmingham, saw in the French Revolution 'the extinction of all national prejudice and enmity, and the establishment of universal peace and good will among all nations.'[16] Another British radical, the Reverend Richard Price, enthusiastically welcomed the Revolution in a sermon and pamphlet in which he said that 'love of our country' should not cause Britons to forget their 'wider obligations as "citizens of the world."'[17] A spirit of world citizenship was not the monopoly of Paine, and on the eve of the publication of his *Rights of Man* the British reformers seemed prepared to embrace international alliances for the cause of world liberty.

The radicals' aspiration for world unity was delivered a sharp and scathing critique by Edmund Burke's *Reflections on the Revolution in France.* Although never a *radical* reformer, Burke had sympathized with the American struggle for direct representation at Westminster. Formerly, he had believed Europe to be a morally and intellectually unified civilization bound together by a common inheritance of classical traditions in culture and learning. But in the *Reflections* Burke emphasized the uniqueness of English political institutions and intellectual evolution, resisting the British Jacobins' 'manifest design of connecting the affairs of France with those of England.'[18] Burke was possessed of a mood of xenophobic retreat. He was at pains to disassociate the political experiment of the French from the Glorious Revolution of 1688 in Britain; he understood the latter as a peculiarly British reform upheld by the British philosopher Locke, and peaceably carried out in response to the unconstitutional behavior of James II. The French Revolution, on the other hand, was seen by Burke as universal in ambition, and as peculiarly French in its impetuosity.

Paine's reply to Burke in *Rights of Man* emphasized the universal character of natural rights, rejecting national interpretations of justice, equality, and the objects of government. The British Jacobins were at first elated to have this alternative declaration of the rights of man and of the first principles of government, but much of their attention was directed to the secondary and illustrative issues raised by Paine, namely his attacks on borough-mongering, the national debt, and the running of political interference by the higher clergy. The British radicals interpreted *Rights of Man* in a peculiarly British context – as a guide for the reform of abuses in their own government and economy. It is partly for this reason that Part II of *Rights of Man* outsold Part I.[19] The former text concentrates upon specific economic and social problems of the 1790s, such as enclosure, unemployment, and poverty, proposing solutions in the form of family allowances, old-age pensions, and tax reductions for the poor. Many of the principles and much of the revolutionary program of Part I, on the other hand, were ignored or even repudiated by the British radicals. They did not follow Paine's advice to leave off veneration for Saxon models of liberty and democracy. They ignored Paine's declaration that the dead have no claim on the institutions of the living. They even opposed Paine's republicanism as an un-British innovation. Providing that Parliament was free of sinecurists and placemen, they preferred a balanced constitution of King, Lords, and Commons. Finally, much of *Rights of Man* generated no debate whatever in British radical circles, including Paine's appeal for an ideological alliance between Britain, France, and the United States, his call for a European Congress to arbitrate international disputes, and his proposal for a worldwide assembly of nations.[20]

As the French Revolutionaries ascended into war with the rest of Europe, the British Jacobins retreated from internationalism and world citizenship. They followed the path carved by the British working class, which at once celebrated Paine's economic proposals and denounced the French as frog-eaters, wearers of wooden shoes, and as effeminate in character. For the British worker the utility of radicalism lay in its capacity to assure them access to roast beef, plum pudding, and beer. The government stoked these patriotic embers at the same time as it portrayed Paine as a traitor and enemy of things British. Even before Paine's trial in 1792, he was being burned and slaughtered in effigy by working people.[21] The Jacobin leaders said little in Paine's defense even when he was tried and convicted *in absentia* for seditious libel.

Late in 1792, Paine re-located to revolutionary France. There he was widely acclaimed by the common people. He would even be awarded honorary citizenship in the new Republic. On the strength of his defense of the Revolution and of world republicanism he was elected to the National Convention. All appeared well. Although a foreigner with a limited knowledge of the French language, Paine provided the French with a degree of international endorsement of their new political regime.

In America and England Paine had managed to avoid factional association, but in France he moved in Girondin circles, especially with Brissot and Cordorcet.[22] This was a natural gravitation for Paine. The Girondins perceived themselves as citizens of the world; they were cosmopolitan in culture, and ardent admirers of the American revolutionaries; and like Paine they wished to export the Revolution immediately. The Jacobins, on the other hand, were not world citizens. As France went to war with Europe, they manifested a growing distrust of foreigners. For the Jacobins the Revolution was an affair of the French nation. From their point of view it was essential to consolidate the

Revolution at home and to ensure the welfare of the French working class before steering the Revolution abroad.

As the Jacobins moved into the ascendancy in the Convention, it grew clear to Paine that the French Revolution would not, at least in the foreseeable future, evolve into a world revolution. His world vision had again become a liability, and in 1793 he was charged with treason and imprisoned as a foreigner.

The Jacobins were not unjustified in their fear of foreigners, especially in the wake of the King's solicitation of foreign assistance against the Revolution. But Paine they misunderstood. The Jacobins observed his vote against the execution of Louis XVI, forgetting that he was among the first to suggest that France discard its monarchy. Similarly, they observed his English tongue, forgetting that he had long since abjured his loyalty to the British Crown. There was even a degree of mistrust of Paine as an American, especially as the United States maintained a course of neutrality during the French Revolutionary War.

This was the beginning of the end for Paine. He was suffered to remain in prison without significant protest from the American minister in France, Gouverneur Morris. Morris's successor, James Monroe, would eventually secure Paine's release by claiming him as an American citizen, but not before Paine composed forty pages of legalistic argument in demonstration of his American citizenship.[23] It is indeed ironic that Paine, in order to obtain his release from jail, and to remove the threat of the guillotine, was reduced to seeking asylum in a national citizenship.

When Paine returned to America in 1802, he found his citizenship to be of nominal worth only. He was accused by some of having abandoned America,[24] while others took exception to his critique of the Scriptures in *The Age of Reason*. And as American support for the French Revolution waned, Paine was dismissed as a dangerous and un-Christian demagogue. According to the anti-Jacobin pamphleteer William Cobbett, 'men will learn to express all that is base, malignant, treacherous, unnatural and blasphemous, by the single mono-syllable, Paine.'[25]

Paine was alternatively reviled and ignored as he lived out his last years. A great exception was President Jefferson, who still shared much of Paine's world vision. But even Jefferson thought it wise to distance himself from Paine's internationalism and deism.

In England, Paine's name was similarly reviled. He had been declared outside the law in 1792, and in 1798 his name became almost unspeakable for proposing to the Directory a plan for a French invasion of the British Isles. In 1804, he published a pamphlet wishing Napoleon success in this venture.[26] Of course, Paine was of the thinking that Napoleon would install in Britain a democratic republic, and that Britain could then join America and France in disseminating republicanism and world peace. The British, however, were not ready for republicanism. As the patriotic song 'The Sons of Albion' put it:

> Neither rebels, French, sans culottes,
> Nor dupes of tyranny boast,
> Shall conquer the English, the Irish, the Scotch
> Nor shall land upon our coast.[27]

Paine's last desperate plea for world citizenship was made through his scheme for a world religion of benevolent humanity. He outlined a new universal religion of reason in an attempt to unite all humanity.[28] This attack on conventional Christianity made Paine anathema to most of his remaining friends in the United States, including world citizens such as Joseph Priestley.

Paine was the victim of a conservative religious reaction in America, which witnessed a growing ecclesiastical intolerance and fundamentalism. At the same time, the enlightened universalism of the days of the Revolution were degenerating into a new territorial and economic nationalism. It was manifested in militancy (in the case of the War of 1812), and later in imperialism, dressed in the guise of 'manifest destiny.'

This was not Paine's vision. He was possessed of a single-state messianism. At times he seemed willing to have America or France serve as ideological sponsor for the new world union, but the liberty, equality, and peacefulness of all peoples within such a world state had to be respected and ensured. Almost certainly Paine would have viewed the nineteenth and twentieth centuries as sorry failures in attaining this object. His aspirations for the world, however, can still inspire us all.

David Braff

The Forgotten Founding Father: The Impact of Thomas Paine

Thomas Paine must be considered to be one of the world's most unique personalities. From humble beginnings he rose to occupy center stage in the greatest events of his time. Slandered, libeled, and vilified by the most powerful individuals and institutions of his day, he nevertheless succeeded in placing before the world his agenda for freedom, for justice, and for the institution of governments whose purpose is to *serve the governed.*

Impact on the American Revolution

If the America of 1776 and the France of 1789 were tinderboxes, then Thomas Paine was their spark. As a genius communicator to the common man of both countries, he was 'A swayer of public opinion who used his pen with consummate skill to incite decisive action.'[29] Paine possessed that rarest of gifts – an original mind. There is a curious remark in an early pamphlet which admirably expresses his method: 'When precedents fail to assist us, we must return to the first principles of things for information and THINK, as if we were the FIRST MEN that thought.'[30]

When Paine wrote his famous *Common Sense*, the prevailing attitude in the colonies was that 'independence' was a word not to be spoken. Even John Adams called independence 'A hobgoblin of so frightful mien that it would throw a delicate person into fits to look it in the face.'[31] Dr. Benjamin Rush, a major figure of the times, told Paine that 'there were two words which he should avoid by every means necessary for his own safety and that of the public – INDEPENDENCE and REPUBLICANISM.'[32] Yet Paine, consistently willing to endanger himself for the causes in which he believed, published *Common Sense* at his own expense. '*Common Sense* came off the press on January 10, 1776. The fifty-page pamphlet sold more than five hundred thousand copies within a few months (to a population of three million). More than any other single publication, *Common Sense* paved the way for the Declaration of Independence.'[33]

Within six months of its publication, the call for independence, which previously had only been whispered in private, was unanimously ratified by the colonials (July 4, 1776). Not only was Paine the first to publicly call for independence and republican government in the United States, he did the same in France. And the result was no less far reaching.

Impact on the French Revolution

In 1791, the National Assembly controlled France. However, it was as yet unclear as to how the revolution was to proceed, and what form of government should be created. On June 20 of that year, King Louis XVI and his family secretly abandoned Paris and attempted to flee the country. The King's attempted abdication threw France into even greater turmoil.

Once again, Paine led the vanguard. He composed a manifesto calling for the formation of a republic in France before anyone else had even hinted at the idea. On July 1, he raced through the streets of Paris plastering the proclamation wherever people would gather. Again, an idea which had barely been whispered was now cleared for open discussion. The establishment of the French Republic, based upon the *Declaration of the Rights of Man and of Citizens* (which Paine co-authored), was soon to follow. Such was the power of Thomas Paine's pen.

The Right of the Individual

Paine was ever ready to lend his talents to the cause of individuals as well as the mass of humanity. In one of the most moving episodes of the revolution, Paine worked to save the life of a British officer, Captain Asgill. Asgill was to be executed by the Americans in reprisal for the hanging of an American, Captain Huddy of the Jersey Militia, who had been executed without warrant or justification. Paine, in his *A Supernumerary Crisis* (May 31, 1782), placed the responsibility for Huddy and Asgill squarely on the shoulders of the British, and privately wrote to Washington urging that he spare Asgill's life. When Marie Antoinette wrote to the same purpose, Asgill was released. Thus, to Paine, even the lives of enemies were worth saving when principles of justice were involved.

It was in his defense of the life of King Louis that we see the clearest possible example of Paine's courage and dedication to the rights of the individual. 'There is little doubt that Paine worked harder than any other member of the Convention to save the life of Louis XVI.'[34] 'Bertrand De Moleville, an ardent royalist and implacable enemy of republicanism who took refuge in England during the trial, gave Paine the highest tribute for his speech in the monarch's favor. He considered it "to the eternal shame of the Assembly that Thomas Paine, misguided by the fanaticism of the most ardent demagogery, was the most wise, the most humane, the most courageous, in a word, the least culpable of all his colleagues."' … 'This [the defense of Louis XVI] was in a sense the most dramatic crisis in Paine's life.'[35]

Despite the furious outbursts of Marat and Thuriot, and risking the ire of Robespierre, despite the ominous sounds of the guillotine doing its grisly work, Paine spoke out. 'With his dogged sincere purpose and faith in human benevolence, he was attempting to withstand the forces of dissent and protest which had been building up for generations. As usual, Paine pleased nobody. The Girondins ignored his appeal for mercy. The Jacobins condemned him as a sentimental tool of the Girondins, and the English reviled him as a regicide enemy merely because of his presence in the Convention.'[36] Paine's defense of the king led to his own imprisonment. His rationality, his reason, and his commitment to rights and justice had no place in a revolution which had begun to devour its own. Paine spent nearly a year in the Luxembourg prison while hundreds, then thousands were killed. It was only through a twist of fate that Paine, whose death warrant had been signed by Robespierre, was not executed.

Paine on Religion: *The Age of Reason*

The irony of Paine being reviled for his well-meant words and actions was not limited to his defense of the king. *The Age of Reason*, Paine's most controversial work, was undertaken in part as a response to the atheism of the French Revolutionists. That Paine should have ultimately been accused of and reviled for being an atheist himself is the height of injustice. Paine himself was an ardent deist; he believed strongly in a Creator, an afterlife, the need to do good and to repent sin.[37] However, being raised as a Quaker, he had a strong aversion to orthodox Christianity and the actions of the established churches. *The Age of Reason* stated these thoughts in a way that proved to be quite unpopular. 'The key to Heaven is not in the keeping of any sect, nor ought the road to it be obstructed by any. Our relation to each other in the *world* is as *men*, and the man who is a friend to *man*, and to his rights, let his religious opinions be what they may, is a good citizen.'[38] As [Vernon] Parrington states in his Pulitzer Prize-winning *Main Currents in American Thought*, 'To the animosity which his political principles excited among the Federalists, was added the detestation of the orthodox for the deism of *The Age of Reason*. The ministers outdid the politicians in virulent attacks upon his reputation, until the generous Quaker, the friend of humanity, and citizen of the world, was shrunk and distorted, into 'The Infidel Tom Paine.' It was a strange reward for a life spent in service to mankind. Like all idealists, he made the mistake of underestimating the defensive strength of vested interests and their skill in arousing mob prejudice.'[39]

That Paine should have suffered for his views is understandable. *The Age of Reason* attacked the authority of the establishment. But it is those slanderous comments based on ignorance, like those of Teddy Roosevelt, who called Paine a 'filthy little atheist,' having never read his works, which soil and cling to Paine's reputation, even to today.

The Legacy of Reason

Thomas Paine wrote that reason, like time, makes its own way.[40] In this, he has been proven wrong. Paine has been largely forgotten by the two governments in whose formation he played such an important part. There are no Thomas Paine high schools, libraries, scholarships, and so forth, and this is a great injustice. But Paine also said that 'time makes more converts than reason,'[41] and, fortunately, this has proven to be true. Paine's ideas on individual rights and the role of government in society, which so shocked the ruling order in his day, seem today to be both obvious and correct.

'In the political realm, his principles are now considered axiomatic – and for that reason, no longer associated with him. The universal acceptance of his principles has paradoxically meant the decline of his popularity, for the degree to which they have been accepted and applied in society, they have lost the aura of novelty and individuality.'[42]

Paine is important today, not only for his defiance of existing institutions but because of the modern cast of his mind. Paine gave us a belief in the possibility of changing the shape of existing governments and the course of entire nations to accommodate the needs of the living.

Paine has left us a very considerable legacy. More than any other individual, he provides us with the vocabulary and frame of reference of modern political thought. Upon his death, most newspapers of the day reprinted the obituary notice from the *New York Citizen*, which read in part, 'He lived long, did some good and much harm.' How poorly understood were his ideas and their impact on the world both then and now. 'His views have been claimed by people anywhere who desire to form for themselves a government which gives to every individual a just measure of liberty.'[43]

And so the spirit of Thomas Paine, his headstone shattered, his grave robbed, lives on in declarations of independence and constitutions creating representative governments by and for the people, worldwide. Thomas Paine, who, until the age of 37, was a complete failure, demonstrates what a single individual can accomplish. Once he found his true calling, he proved that neither kings nor armies nor governments can withstand the 'power of an idea whose time has come.'

Eric Foner

Thomas Paine and American Radicalism during the American Revolution

Of the men who made the American Revolution, none had a more remarkable career, or suffered a more peculiar fate, than Thomas Paine. While his friends, Thomas Jefferson and George Washington, and his ideological antagonist John Adams, came from middle-and upper-class families long established on American soil, Paine's origins lay among the 'lower orders' of eighteenth-century England, and he did not even arrive in America until the very eve of the revolutionary war. Unlike Alexander Hamilton, another leader of the Revolution born abroad, Paine always remained something of an outsider in America. He never developed true local roots here – as he once told Benjamin Franklin, 'where liberty is not, there is my country.' Paine's profound influence on American events was acknowledged by friends and opponents alike, but after his death, he was excluded from the group of revolutionary leaders canonized in American popular culture. His memory was kept alive primarily by succeeding generations of radicals, who rediscovered him again and again as a symbol of revolutionary internationalism, free-thinking, and defiance of existing institutions.

Paine's biographers have always confronted an unenviable task, and not only because of the complexity of Paine's personality and the fact that most of his correspondence and papers were accidentally burned over a century ago. To depict Paine in his entirety requires a knowledge of the history of America, England, and France, as well as of eighteenth-century science, theology, political philosophy and radical movements. Paine's connections must be traced among the powerful in Europe and America, and also in the tavern-centered world of politically-conscious artisans in London and Philadelphia. In fact, the questions central to an understanding of Paine's career lie well beyond the confines of conventional biography. It is perhaps not surprising that while several fine lives of Paine now exist, a great deal of mystery still surrounds his career. Paine's ideas have never been grasped in their full complexity, nor have they been successfully located in the social context of Paine's age. Some writers have isolated individual strands of Paine's thought –

Newtonian science, deism, political egalitarianism, the promotion of business enterprise and economic growth – as the 'key' to Paine's thought, but no one has shown how, why, and when these various strands became integrated into the coherent ideology of which, for Paine at least, they were component parts. Neither the roots of Paine's thought, nor the reasons for the tremendous impact of his writings in America and Europe have been fully explained. And Paine's exact relationship is still not clear, to the expansion of popular participation in politics, the politicization of the 'lower orders,' which was among the revolutionary achievements of the Age of Revolution.[44]

Obviously, it would be impossible in a brief paper to resolve the many questions which still revolve around the life of this enigmatic figure. But it should be possible to consider what made Paine unique as a radical pamphleteer of the late eighteenth century, and to analyze the essential assumptions of his republican thought. Most writers would be happy to produce one work of significance and popularity in a lifetime; Paine wrote three pamphlets which were among the greatest best-sellers of his age – *Common Sense*, *Rights of Man*, and *The Age of Reason*. Many of the successes and failures of Paine's career stemmed from his role as a pamphleteer of revolution. One of the most astute contemporary comments on his strengths and weaknesses was made by Madame Roland during the French Revolution.

> The boldness of his thoughts, the originality of his style, the incisive truths, audaciously flung before the very persons they offend, have doubtless produced a great sensation; but I find him more fit, as it were, to scatter these kindling sparks than to lay the foundation or prepare the formation of a government. Paine is better at lighting the way for revolution than drafting a constitution. He grasps, he establishes those great principles whose exposition attracts everyone's attention, ravishing a club and exciting a tavern gathering; but as for dispassionate committee discussion or the day-to-day work of a legislator, I consider [the English reformer] David Williams infinitely more suited than he.[45]

For a variety of reasons which cannot be gone into here, Paine was a failure as a legislator during the French Revolution. But in 1776 in America, and 1791-92 in England, he was precisely the right man at the right time, articulating ideas which were in the air but only dimly perceived by most of his contemporaries. How can we explain this success?

Since Paine's political ideas and literary style remained essentially fixed from *Common Sense* to the end of his career, a brief analysis of Paine's first great pamphlet may help reveal the reasons for his unparalleled achievements as a pamphleteer. Although *Common Sense* is best known for its advocacy of American independence, Paine always considered its argument for republicanism the most important part of the pamphlet. 'The mere independence of America,' he later wrote, 'were it to have been followed by a system of government modeled after the corrupt system of English government, would not have interested me with the unabated ardor it did. It was to bring forward and establish the representative system of government, as the work itself will show, that was the leading principle with me in writing.' Paine's savage attack on 'the so much boasted Constitution of England' contains the most striking passages in *Common Sense*. He denounced the whole notion of the historical legitimacy of the monarchy: 'A French bastard landed with an armed banditti and establishing himself king of England against the consent of the natives, is in plain terms a very paltry rascally original … The plain truth is that the antiquity of the English monarchy will not bear looking into.' Paine minced no words in his assault on the principle of hereditary rule. The House of Lords was simply the 'remains of an aristocratic tyranny' and as for the monarchy: 'Of more worth is one honest man to society, and in the sight of God, than all the crowned ruffians that ever lived.' Paine was the first writer in America to denounce the English constitution so completely, to deny that balanced government was essential to liberty, and to transform the word 'republic' from a term of abuse in political writing – a synonym for Cromwellian dictatorship – to a living political issue and an ideal of government.[46]

Common Sense then turned to a discussion of independence, a subject which had been mentioned sporadically in the press in 1775, but which most colonists still refused to confront – although war with Britain had begun months before and the prospects for reconciliation were dim. Paine's argument again departed from those of previous pamphleteers. Their attacks on British policy had stressed the danger to colonial liberties; Paine gave more emphasis both to economic self-interest and to a vision of an American empire, freed from European domination and trading freely with the entire world. And, in his most lyrical passages, Paine announced the creation of an independent American republic in the language of an impending millennium. 'We have it in our power to begin the world over again,' he declared, '… the birthday of a new world is at hand.' Paine transformed a struggle over the rights of Englishmen into a contest with meaning for all mankind. In a world in which 'every spot of the old world is overrun with oppression,' America would become 'an asylum for mankind.'[47]

The immediate success and impact of *Common Sense* was nothing less than astonishing, as every scholar of the Revolution has agreed. At a time when the average political pamphlet was printed in one or two editions, *Common Sense* went through twenty-five editions in the single year of 1776. But John Adams always resented the idea that the pamphlet contributed much to the movement for independence. Its discussion of that subject, he insisted, was 'a tolerable summary of the arguments which I had been repeating again and again in Congress for nine months.' Nothing in it was new, with the exception of 'the phrases, suitable for an emigrant from New Gate, or one who had chiefly associated with such company, such as "the royal brute of England."' Adams may have been ungrateful, but to some extent he was right. *Common Sense* did express ideas which became fixed parts of American ideology – the separateness of America from Europe, the corruption of the old world and innocence of the new, the virtues of republican government and the absurdity of hereditary privilege – but none of these was original with Paine. What set *Common Sense* apart was its literary tone and style. Its tone, which contemporaries described as 'daring imprudence' and 'uncommon frenzy' was far removed from the legalistic, logical arguments of other American political pamphlets, whose style was 'essentially decorous and reasonable.'[48]

But there was more to Paine's appeal than the enraged assaults on hereditary monarchy which offended Adams, the 'indecent expressions' to which Henry Laurens of South Carolina objected. Paine was the conscious pioneer of a new style of political writing, one designed to extend political discussion beyond the narrow bounds of the eighteenth century's 'political nation.' 'As it is my design to make those that can scarcely read understand,' he once wrote, 'I shall therefore avoid every literary ornament and put it in language as plain as the alphabet.' He assumed knowledge of no authority but the Bible, employed no Latin phrases, or when he did immediately provided translations, and avoided florid language designed to impress more cultivated readers. Paine was capable, to be sure, of creating brilliant metaphors, such as his famous reply to Edmund Burke's sympathy for the fate of Marie Antoinette in *Rights of Man*: 'He pities the plumage, but forgets the dying bird.' But the hallmarks of his writing were clarity, directness, and forcefulness. Paine's rage was tempered by a conscious attempt to engage the reason as well as the passions of his readers. His savage attacks on kingship and his careful exposition of republicanism were two sides of the same coin: both were meant to undermine the entire system of deferential politics. He flaunted his contempt for precedent and authority. 'In this part of the debate,' he wrote in the spring of 1776 of a newspaper antagonist, 'Cato shelters himself chiefly in quotations from other authors, without reasoning much on the matter himself; in answer to which, I present him with a string of maxims and recollections, drawn from the nature of things, without borrowing from anyone.' Paine's message was that anyone could understand the nature of politics and the principles of government – all it took was common sense.[49]

To his critics, Paine was as guilty of degrading the language as of attacking government. Gouverneur Morris scoffed at him as 'a mere adventurer … without fortune, without family or connections, ignorant even of grammar.' But Paine was indeed a conscious artist. Most American pamphleteers before Paine aimed their works at the educated classes, believing that to write for a mass audience meant to sacrifice refinement for coarseness and triviality. Paine's literary style, his rejection of deference, and his political republicanism were all interdependent: for Paine, the medium, in effect, was of one piece with the message.[50]

What of Paine's audience? As a professional pamphleteer, Paine naturally addressed his writings to the widest possible readership in America and England. His works were read, as one contemporary noted, in 'all ranks.' It would be wrong to consider Paine the consistent spokesman for any single social class. His personal and political associations, both in America and Europe, spanned the worlds of the upper-class salon and tavern political debates. Yet Paine's particular brand of republican ideology struck its deepest chords among the artisan class in both England and America. In the late eighteenth century, artisans on both sides of the Atlantic awakened to political consciousness and became carriers of egalitarian political ideas. In America, throughout the revolutionary era, they denounced the pretensions of men of great wealth who had 'the impudence to assert that mechanics are men of no consequence' and 'make no scruples to say that the mechanics ... have no right to be consulted in matters of government.' Thousands of artisans were brought into organized political life via the extra-legal committees created to enforce non-importation in the years preceding independence. In England, the French Revolution and the appearance of Paine's *Rights of Man* helped to stimulate the sudden emergence in the 1790s of the radical corresponding societies, rooted in the artisan communities of London and provincial industrial centers like Sheffield and Leeds, which demanded an expansion of political rights to the mass of English citizens.[51]

This class just emerging into political consciousness found its voice in Paine's writings. Paine literally created for it a new political language, redefining the meaning of old words like republic and democracy, using them repeatedly in a favorable, rather than derogatory, sense. Alone among the major pamphleteers of this period, Paine had sprung from the very mass audience which so eagerly devoured his writings. He had begun life as an artisan, following his father's trade of staymaking before turning to the excise service. His first thirty-seven years, spent in England, had been spent among the lower middle class of artisans, lesser professional men and petty government officials, and in centers of political disaffection like London and Lewes. The anti-British rage expressed in *Common Sense* may well reflect the disappointment of such men of talent in a society characterized by hereditary privilege and patronage politics.[52]

As his recent biographer David Hawke writes, Paine not only retained a manual agility with tools throughout his life, but remained 'a city man at heart.' Though he shared Jefferson's democratic egalitarianism, Paine had little in common with the agrarian bias of Jefferson's thought. Jefferson hoped America could insulate itself against the industrial revolution and regarded commercial banks and a national debt as elements of corruption. Paine was enchanted by the cotton mills, potteries, and steel furnaces of England in the 1780s and hoped such enterprises could be 'carried on in America as well.' He defended the Bank of North America against its opponents in Pennsylvania politics in the mid-1780s, and in *Common Sense* favored the creation of a national debt as a 'national bond.'[53]

Paine's blend of democratic egalitarianism and enthusiasm for business enterprise was shared by his artisan audience. The artisan was part workingman, part property-holding petty entrepreneur. The Philadelphia artisans among whom Paine circulated during his American career were ardent supporters of the ultra-democratic Pennsylvania constitution of 1776 – which Paine also defended in a series of newspaper articles – but as city dwellers they saw the Bank of North America as a bulwark of a stable, noninflationary currency, and as small businessmen they desired a stronger central government which could promote manufacture and trade.[54]

In America and England, artisans responded with enthusiasm to Paine's assault on established political institutions, his attack on the principle of hereditary privilege, his assertion that every man of common sense could understand the nature of government. They found extremely congenial Paine's anti-aristocratic ethos, his glorification of the 'producing classes' as opposed to the idle rich. 'Why ... does Mr. Burke,' Paine asked in *Rights of Man*, 'talk of this House of Peers, as the pillar of the landed interest? Were that pillar to sink into the earth, the same landed property would continue, and the same plowing, sowing, and reaping would go on. The aristocracy are not the farmers who work the land and raise the produce, but ... are the drones ... who neither collect the honey nor form the hive, but exist only for lazy enjoyment.'[55] Such an outlook not only resonated with resentments against political privilege and the lavish lifestyle of the rich, which artisans on both sides of the Atlantic shared, but it also expressed a view of social conflict as a struggle between producers and non-producers (rather than employers and employees, or rich and poor), which would strongly influence the course of radical thought well into the nineteenth century.

Paine's radicalism, after all, did not extend to an attack on the institution of private property. In *Common Sense*, he attributed economic distinctions and inequalities of wealth to differences in talent, industry, and frugality among individuals. 'The distinctions of rich and poor,' he declared, 'may in a great measure be accounted for ... without recourse to the harsh ill-sounding names of oppression and avarice. Oppression is often the *consequence*, but seldom or never the *means* of riches.' Indeed, what impressed Paine about America was its egalitarian distribution of property and high standard of living compared with the old world. 'There are not three millions of people in any part of the universe,' Paine wrote in 1782, 'who live so well, or have such a fund of ability, as in America.' And in *Rights of Man* he declared, 'I see in America, the generality of the people living in a style of plenty unknown in monarchial countries; and I see that the principle of its government, which is that of the equal rights of man, is making rapid progress in the world.' This association between economic abundance and republican government was a crucial element in Paine's social outlook and helps explain why he did not attribute inequalities of wealth to economic oppression. Indeed, Paine's republican utopianism left little room for class or social conflict of any kind. Both class and party conflict were, in a sense, incompatible with the nature of republicanism which, according to Paine, 'does not admit of an interest distinct from that of the nation.'[56]

Unlike Madison and other republican thinkers who viewed men as motivated basically by selfish interests and believed the only way to preserve liberty was to create a governmental structure balancing competing ambitions and interests, Paine was utterly optimistic about human nature. 'Man,' he wrote, 'were he not corrupted by governments, is naturally the friend of man, and ... human nature is not of itself vicious.' It was men like Madison and John Adams, not Paine, who had a more realistic view of the possibilities of class conflict in a republic. Madison and Adams worked to create a governmental structure which could defuse or neutralize class conflict in the society. Paine was indifferent to the details of frames of government, although he generally preferred a unicameral legislature to represent the unitary interest of a homogenous republican people.[57]

Paine was, to be sure, an eloquent and scathing critic of the social order of Europe. He could comment in moving terms on 'the mass of wretchedness' lying 'hidden from the eye of common observation' and which had 'scarcely any other chance than to expire in poverty or infamy.' Paine shared the artisan's sense of separateness from the eighteenth-century poor, but what he really despised was not the poor, but poverty. In the second part of *Rights of Man*, Paine developed an extensive social welfare program, including an early social security and unemployment relief system, free public education, and the use of progressive taxation to foster economic equality. He helped to provide the link – previously missing in English republican writings (as Professor [Caroline] Robbins has shown) – between demands for political reform and the bitter social grievances of the English lower classes. But Paine never suggested that his plan was applicable to America, because his essential diagnosis of social problems was political. The 'mass of wretchedness' in English society implied that 'something must be wrong in the system of government.' Paine could speak of a republic as socially harmonious because republican government would cut the aristocracy off from its sources of income – hereditary privilege, court sinecures, governmental favors – and would allow full reign to the natural laws of civil society which, Paine believed, would ensure an economic abundance in which all classes would share.[58]

As Professor [J. R.] Pole has shown in an incisive brief analysis of the London Corresponding Society, Paine's view of the relationship between political and social reform strongly influenced the radical movement of the 1790s in England. The radical societies shared Paine's utopian vision of America – only the most radical figure of the movement, John Thelwell, believed that America was 'somewhat short of the true sansculotte liberty,' since Americans 'have too much veneration for property, too much religion, and too much law.' The societies adopted Paine's utter contempt for the existing English political institutions, and his vision of the social harmony which would result from political reform. The social grievances of the LCS and its kindred societies were far deeper than those of the artisan associations and Democratic-Republican societies of contemporary America – a reflection of the differences between the stage of economic development and class structure of the two nations. Every contemporary account of the origins of the English societies stresses that what led the members into political speculation was economic grievances: 'the miserable and wretched state the people were reduced to,' 'the numerous, burthensome and unnecessary taxes,' the 'oppressive game laws and destructive monopolies,' and other causes of 'the lower classes sinking into poverty, disgrace, and excesses.' But in typical Paineite fashion, these social ills were attributed to defects in the political system and, as the LCS explained in 1792, 'reform and abuse' – the inequitable state of Parliamentary representation and the suffrage – 'and the others will all disappear.'[59]

For reasons which are far too complex to be gone into in detail, the writings of Paine became a 'foundation-text' of working-class radicalism in nineteenth-century England, while in America he was all but forgotten after his death.[60] To over-simplify a complex question, Paine's attack on

Christianity and the Bible in *The Age of Reason* (published in the mid-1790s), alienated him not only from the conservative Calvinist clergy, but from the radical Jeffersonian sects as well. Secularism and anti-clericalism became a major strand in English radical thought, but only a minor side issue in America, partially because, after the Revolution, there was no established church to attack, and partly because the institutional church, far from being a bastion of the existing order as in Paine's Europe, was the source of much of the reforming fervor in nineteenth-century America. In the United States, far more critics of society would speak the language of evangelical Protestantism than that of deist rationalism. The irony is that in England, where Paine's political ideals remained unrealized in the nineteenth century, Paine remained a hero to radicals, while Americans who enjoyed republicanism, equality before the laws, and had no titled nobility or hereditary monarch, reviled or ignored Paine. What set him apart was his 'sin' of infidelity, or, perhaps, the poor judgment of having returned to the United States in 1802 in the midst of a religious revival and at the outset of a century characterized above all by its intense religiosity.

Nonetheless, while a continuous 'Paineite' radical tradition has not existed in America, Paine had been rediscovered again and again by American social critics. What makes Paine's radicalism relevant for later generations is not simply, or primarily, the specific tenets of his belief, but his essential cast of mind – his impatience with the past, his bitter contempt for institutions which could not stand the test of reason, his belief that men could shape their own destiny.

Paine's career, in conclusion, might lead us to rethink some of our usual definitions of radicalism in the era of the American Revolution. In a period which in so many ways witnessed the birth of the modern world, Paine was a truly modern figure. His radicalism differed from that of many of his contemporaries in that he had little interest in the past and unbounded optimism about the future. He accepted fully the modern ideas of the perfectibility of man and of unlimited progress. He could not have cared less about the Anglo-Saxon past idealized and used as a model of good government by English radicals, and he did not share the nostalgia of Americans in the Jeffersonian tradition, for an agrarian, pre-capitalist world. He viewed commerce and economic development not as elements of corruption, but as fostering interdependence among men and nations, stimulating all forms of economic enterprise, and lifting the concerns of mankind from the parochial to the cosmopolitan.

Paine embraced fully the fundamental transformations which American society underwent during the era of the American Revolution – the rapid growth of capitalist institutions and social relations, and the vast expansion of political participation to men previously outside the 'political nation.' Many men 'radical' in their political outlook were 'conservative' or at least nostalgic in opposing capitalist development in America; others, like the great merchant Robert Morris, were perhaps 'radical' in being agents of massive social change, but were extremely elitist in their view of politics. But in both the political and economic realms, Paine accepted, in an almost millennial frame of mind, the positive virtues of total change, and he invented a literary style and political language expressing this vision for a new mass audience. Even John Adams had to admit in 1806, 'I know not whether any man in the world has had more influence on its inhabitants or affairs for the last thirty years than Tom Paine.'[61]

Charles Francisco

Thomas Paine: A Most Un-Common Man

> I have never yet made it the least point of consideration whether a thing is popular or unpopular, but whether it is right or wrong.
> *A Friend to Rhode-Island and the Union*, 1783

Thomas Paine wrote those words in 1783, at the height of his personal popularity, and he meant exactly what he said. He lived by them through war, political persecution, and imprisonment, and he refused to turn away from them in the face of approaching death. Paine, as we have learned, had risen from humble beginnings to become the most influential writer of his time, and the clarity and strength of his words rallied an era to the cause of freedom. But his uncompromising quest to enlighten the world through reason and common sense would, perhaps inevitably, place his own reputation in jeopardy. He would fall from hero to outcast. And as we have learned, at his death, a New York obituary remarked that he had 'done some good, and much harm,' and an American president would later dismiss him as 'a filthy little atheist.'

It has always been my belief that Tom Paine's own words afford the strongest defense against his harshest critics, past and present. With that in mind, it is appropriate that we spend a few short minutes *hearing* the actual words of this brilliant man of the eighteenth century. Time restrictions have prompted my presumptuous editing to extract only a few key passages from his work.

Thomas Paine arrived in the New World in 1774, and he was soon hired as editor of *Pennsylvania Magazine*. Even then he was determined to 'do some good for mankind.' Some of his earliest articles dared to criticize a variety of then-accepted oppressions:

> ON SLAVERY. 'Ever since the discovery of America, Britain hath employed herself in the most horrid of all traffics, that of the human flesh … hath yearly ravaged the hapless shores of Africa, robbing it of its unoffending inhabitants to cultivate her stolen Dominions to the West … When the Almighty shall have blest us and made us a people dependent only upon Him, then may our first gratitude be shown by an act of legislation which shall put a stop to the importance of negroes for sale, soften the hard fate of

those already there, and in time procure their freedom.'
'African Slavery in America,' *Pennsylvania Journal*, March 1775

ON WOMEN. 'Surrounded on all sides by judges who are at once their tyrants and seducers, who does not feel for the tender sex? If a woman were to defend the cause of her sex, she might address him in the following manner: "How great is your injustice. If we have an equal right with you to virtue, why should we not have a right to praise? The public esteem ought to wait upon merit ... Why must we be condemned to die unknown? Deny us not the public esteem which, after the esteem of one's self, is the sweetest reward of well doing."'
Pennsylvania Magazine, edited by Paine, 1775-1776

ON PACIFISM. 'I am thus far a Quaker that I would gladly agree with all the world to lay aside the use of arms, and settle matters by negotiations; but, unless the whole [world] will, the matter ends, and I take up my musket and thank heaven He has put it in my power. We live not in a world of angels.'
Pennsylvania Magazine, edited by Paine 1775-1776

Paine had been in America only six months when a series of bloody skirmishes broke out between British soldiers and American colonists. A few had talked of American independence but none dared go on record as supporting it in the public print, except for Tom Paine. In January of 1776, at his own expense, he published his remarkable *Common Sense*:

> Some writers have so confounded society with government as to leave little or no distinction between them ... Society is produced by our wants, and government by our wickedness; the former promotes our happiness *positively* by uniting our affections, the latter *negatively* by restraining our vices. Society in every state is a blessing, but government, even in its best state, is but a necessary evil ... Government, like dress, is the badge of lost innocence ... Mankind being originally equal in the order of creation, the equality could only be destroyed by some subsequent circumstance ... Nothing in nature or religion could allow for the distinction of men into kings and subjects ... so far as we approve of monarchy ... in America *the law is king* ... Everything that is right or natural pleads for separation. The blood of the slain, the

weeping voice of nature cries, *'Tis time to part* ... Every quiet method for peace has been ineffectual ... A Government of our own is our natural right ... O! Ye that love mankind! Ye that dare oppose not only the tyranny but the tyrant, stand forth! Every spot of the Old World is overrun with oppression. Freedom hath been hunted around the globe. Asia and Africa have long expelled her. Europe regards her like a stranger, and England hath given her warning to depart. O! Receive the fugitive, and prepare in time an asylum for mankind. The cause of America is in great measure the cause of all mankind. 'Tis not the concern of a day, a year, or an age; posterity are virtually involved in the contest and will be more or less affected, even to the end of time, by the proceedings now.

Common Sense, January 10, 1776

The success of *Common Sense* could have made Paine a wealthy man, but he turned over his lucrative royalties to the Continental Congress, resigned from his job, and enlisted as a private in the Continental Army. The bright July dreams of independence turned to despair during the cruel winter of 1776, and Paine picked up his stronger weapon, the pen, to fan the flame of hope anew in *The American Crisis*:

These are the times that try men's souls. The summer soldier and the sunshine patriot will, in this crisis, shrink from the service of their country; but he that stands it *now* deserves the love and thanks of man and woman. Tyranny, like hell, is not easily conquered; yet we have this consolation with us, that the harder the conflict, the more glorious the triumph. What we obtain too cheap we esteem too lightly ... Heaven knows how to put a proper price on its goods; and it would be strange indeed if so celestial an article as FREEDOM should not be highly rated ... Tis the business of little minds to shrink; but he whose heart is firm, and whose conscience approves his conduct, will pursue his principles unto death ... By perseverance and fortitude we have the prospect of a glorious issue; by cowardice and submission, the sad choice of a variety of evils – a ravaged country – a depopulated city – habitations without safety, and slavery without hope ... Look on this picture and weep over it! ... I call not upon a few, but upon all: not on *this* state or *that* state, but on *every* state: up and help us; lay your shoulders to the wheel ... Let it be

told to the future world, that in the depth of winter, when nothing but hope and virtue could survive, that the city and the country, alarmed at one common danger, came forth to meet and repulse it.
The American Crisis I, December 19, 1776

And he continued to address vital issues in his *Crisis Papers* throughout the long struggle for American independence:

If we attend the nature of freedom, we shall see the proper way of treating her ... The ancients lost her because they tried so hard to bolt and cage her. An injudicious security becomes her prison and, disgusted with captivity, she becomes an exile. Freedom is the associate of innocence, not the companion of suspicion. She only requires to be *cherished*, not to be caged. And to be loved is, to her, to be protected. She connects herself with man as God made him, not as fortune altered him, and continues with him to be just and civil ...

'The times that tried men's soul' are over ... To see it in our power to make a world happy, to teach mankind the art of being so, to exhibit on the theatre of the universe a character hitherto unknown, and to have, as it were, a new creation entrusted in our hands are honors that command reflection and can neither be too highly estimated nor too gratefully received. It would be a circumstance ever to be lamented and never to be forgotten were a single blot ... suffered to fall on a revolution which to the end of time must be an honor to the age that accomplished it, and which has contributed more to enlighten the world and diffuse a spirit of freedom and liberality among mankind than any human event ... that ever preceded it.
The American Crisis XIII, April 19, 1783

With independence won, Paine's need to earn a living took him to Europe, and his arrival coincided with the eruption of the French Revolution. Edmund Burke's attack on that revolution, coupled with his defense of the British monarchy, prompted Paine to write his next great work, *Rights of Man*.

The end of all political associations is the preservation of the natural and imprescriptible rights of man; and these rights are liberty, property, security, and resistance of oppression ... The Nation is essentially the source of all sovereignty; nor can any individual or any body of men be entitled to any authority which is not expressly derived from it.

    There never did, nor can exist a parliament, or any description of man, or any generation of men in any country, possessed of the right or the power of binding or controlling posterity to 'the end of time.' ... Every age and generation must be free to act for itself ... as the ages and generations which preceded it. The vanity and presumption of governing beyond the grave, is the most ridiculous and insolent of all tyrannies ... I am not contending for, nor against, any form of government, nor for nor against any party, here or elsewhere ... I am contending for, the right of the *living*, and against their being willed away, and controlled and contracted for, by the manuscript-assumed authority of the dead ...

    A constitution is not a thing in name only, but in fact. It has not an ideal, but a real existence; and wherever it cannot be produced in a visible form, there is none. A constitution is a thing antecedent to a government, and the government is only the creature of a constitution ... It is the body of elements, to which you can refer, and quote article by article ... A constitution, therefore, is to a government, what the laws ... are to a court ... The court ... does not make the laws, neither can it alter them; it only acts in conformity to the laws made; and the government is in like manner governed by the constitution.

Rights of Man Part I, 1791

Paine's new book was enthusiastically received by a majority of the British people, but the government quickly moved to suppress it and eventually tried to arrest the author for sedition. Paine fled to France where he was greeted as a hero, made an honorary citizen, and elected to the National Convention. In that position, he was faced again with a choice of 'right or wrong.' As he saw it, despite his long abhorrence of the monarchy, he made a futile plea that the life of the deposed king be spared.

> I am inclined to believe that if Louis Capet had been born in obscure condition, had he lived within the circle of an amiable and respectable neighborhood, at liberty to practice the duties of domestic life, had he been thus situated, I cannot believe that he would have shown himself destitute of social virtues ... It is to

France alone, I know, that the United States of America owe that support which enabled them to shake off the unjust and tyrannical yoke of Britain ... Let then those United States be the safeguard and asylum of Louis Capet. There, hereafter, far removed from the miseries and crimes of royalty, he may learn, from the constant aspect of public prosperity, that the true system of government consists not in kings, but in fair, equal and honorable representation ...

Reasons for Preserving the Life of Louis Capet,
Address to French National Convention, January 15, 1793

Thomas Paine's reasoned defense of the king turned those who led the French reign of terror against him. He was not surprised, as he revealed in a letter to Samuel Adams in America:

It has been my intention, for several years past, to publish my thoughts upon religion ... my friends were falling as fast as the guillotine could cut their heads off, and as I expected every day the same fate, I resolved to begin my work ... The people of France were running headlong into atheism, and I had the work translated in their own language, to stop them in that career, and fix them to the first article of every man's creed who has any creed at all and that first article should be – *I believe in God.*

Letter to Samuel Adams, January 1, 1803

And, on his way to a French prison, he turned over the first pages of a manuscript that he would complete during his incarceration. He dedicated *The Age of Reason* to the American people.

TO MY FELLOW CITIZENS OF THE UNITED STATES OF AMERICA.

I put the following work under your protection. It contains my opinions on religion. You will do me justice to remember that I have always strenuously supported the right of every man to his own opinion, however different that opinion might be from mine. He who denies to another this right, makes a slave of himself to his present opinion, because he precludes himself the right of changing it. The most formidable weapon against errors of every kind is reason. I have never used any other, and I trust I never shall.

> I believe in one God, and no more; and I hope for happiness beyond this life. I believe in the equality of man; and I believe that religious duties consist in doing justice, loving mercy, and endeavoring to make our fellow-creatures happy … My own *mind* is my church … All national … churches, whether Jewish, Christian or Turkish, appear to me to be no other than human inventions, set up to terrify and enslave mankind, and monopolize power and profit … The creation we behold is the real and ever existing Word of God, in which we cannot be deceived. It proclaims His power, it demonstrates His wisdom, it manifests His goodness and beneficence … seeing, as we do daily, the goodness of God (to all His Creatures) is an example calling upon all men to practice the same towards each other …
>
> *The Age of Reason*, Part 1, 1794
>
> My country is the world … my religion is to do good.
>
> *Rights of Man*, Part 2, 1792

Paine's writings had always been controversial, but none provoked the venom that followed the publication of *The Age of Reason*. He answered one attack in a pamphlet called *Agrarian Justice*.

> What has determined me to publish it now is a sermon preached by Watson, Bishop of Llandaff (who) … wrote a book entitled *An Apology for the Bible*, in answer to my second part of *The Age of Reason* … It is wrong to say God made *rich and poor*; He made only *male and female*; and He gave them the earth for their inheritance … Instead of preaching to encourage one part of mankind in insolence … it would be better that priests employed their time to render the general condition of man less miserable than it is.
>
> *Agrarian Justice*, 1797

Prowling British warships made it impossible for Tom Paine to return to his adopted country for fifteen long years. The patriot-philosopher, who had first suggested that the foundling republic he named the United States of America and had first called for a formal Declaration of Independence and a written Constitution, was now shunned by most who had once felt honored to call him friend. But the aging prophet without honor found the strength to continue his fight for a more peaceful world.

In 1803, President Thomas Jefferson received the original draft, in Paine's handwriting, of a visionary proposal he called: *An Association of Nations.*

> It shall be an unarmed Association for the protection of the rights and commerce of nations that shall be neutral in time of war ... The Association shall establish a flag for itself to be carried by every ship and vessel of every nation ... This flag to be a pennant at the head of the mainmast, and it is to be composed of the same colors as compose the rainbow, and arranged in the same order as they appear in that phenomenon ... We, therefore, the powers composing this Association, declare that we will, each one for itself, prohibit in our dominions the exportation or transportation of military stores ... and all kinds of iron and steel weapons used in war.
>
> *Maritime Compact: An Association of Nations*,
> In *To the Citizens of the United States*, Letter 7, published in
> *The National Intelligencer*, April 21, 1803

Unfortunately, nothing came of his plan for an Association of Nations. Thomas Paine died in New York City in 1809 and was buried on his farm in New Rochelle, because the Quaker cemetery would not have him. His grave was robbed some years later and his bones were placed in a fine wooden chest and transported to England. That chest, with his remains inside, was later sold as a piece of furniture and lost forever. Tom Paine left the world as inconspicuously as he had entered it. Of the countless words Thomas Paine wrote extolling the virtues of liberty during a time when that commodity was in very short supply, my personal favorites are these contained in a letter to a New Jersey friend during his long sojourn in Europe. His friend wondered if Paine, so long away, had *forgotten* America.

> A thousand years hence, perhaps in less, America may be what England now is: the innocence of her character that won the hearts of all nations in her favor may sound like a romance, and her inimitable virtue as if it never had been. The ruins of that liberty which thousands bled for or suffered to obtain may just furnish materials for a village tale or extort a sigh from rustic sensibility while the fashionable of that day, enveloped in dissipation, shall deride the principle and deny the fact.

When we contemplate the fall of empires and the extinctions of nations of the Ancient world, we see but little to excite our regret than the mouldering ruins of pompous palaces, magnificent monuments, lofty pyramids, and walls and towers of the most costly workmanship. But when the empire of America shall fall, the subject for contemplative sorrow will be infinitely greater than the crumbling brass or marble can inspire. It will not then be said, here stood a temple of vast antiquity; here rose a Babel of invisible height, or there a palace of sumptuous extravagance. But *here* – ah painful thought, the noblest work of human wisdom, the grandest scene of human glory, the fair cause of freedom rose and fell! Read this and ask if I forget America.

Letter to Mrs. Few of Bordentown*, NJ*, January 6, 1789

Thomas Paine dedicated his life to enlightening the ranks of those his high-born peers called the 'common men.' In decades of fearless work, he never forgot his roots while proving that he was, himself, a most uncommon man. It is singularly appropriate that we remember, in this place, other words his quill scratched out almost 200 years ago:

An army of principles will penetrate where an army of soldiers cannot; it will succeed where diplomatic management would fail: it is neither the Rhine, the Channel, nor the Ocean that can arrest its progress: it will march on the horizon of the world, and it will conquer.

Agrarian Justice, 1797

Bernard Vincent

From Social to International Peace: The Realistic Utopias of Thomas Paine

That Thomas Paine was a pioneer, a prophet, a visionary is something that cannot reasonably be denied. As early as 1778 he defined himself as a 'farmer of thoughts.' But as he was not a man to cultivate ideas for his own private use, he added: 'all the crops I raise I give away.'[62] Thus not only did he coin the phrase 'United States of America,' thereby giving a name to his as yet unchristened adopted country, but he was the first American to mention the idea of a 'declaration of independence,' the first to denounce the sacredness of the King of England, the first to propose a legislative project for the gradual abolition of slavery, the first to advocate national and international copyright, the first (in 1780) to call for the election of 'a Continental Convention for the purpose of forming a Continental constitution,'[63] the first (in 1783) to suggest the establishment of 'a general government over the Union,'[64] and – but I shall go back to this later – the first to plead for international arbitration, the first also (in 1790) to carry the American flag in a foreign procession, the first in revolutionary France to create a republican club, to launch a republican journal and to publish a republican manifesto; and finally, the first to write a scathing criticism of Christianity and the Bible, *not* with a view to promoting atheism but, paradoxically, in order to prevent its expansion.

It seems, however, that Paine has been much less celebrated as a prophet of peace than as a proponent of American Independence or an advocate of human rights or a denouncer of revealed religions. Popular imagery often represents him with a gun in his hands, writing bellicose exhortations by the light of some campfire (which he actually did), and the fact is that he is less frequently depicted as a pacifist than as a warmonger or at least as a Quaker armed to the teeth. In part, this blurred image is, I think, precisely due to his strange relationship with the Society of Friends. All those familiar with the life of Thomas Paine know that his father was a Quaker. Although he never formally belonged to the Society, Paine was deeply influenced by his father's creed and, as a rule, he had more faith in dialogue and persuasion than in violent confrontation. But, for all that, he was too much of a realist ever to subscribe to the naïve or hypocritical ideas of those who, in the name of non-violence, always tend to collaborate with the powers-that-be, however despotic, or, in times of war, to side with the winning camp or, even worse, with the invader. Much like Gandhi, he would have been strongly averse to *unilateral* disarmament. Although a lover of peace, he was no pacifist in the strict sense of the word, persuaded as he was that liberty could not be defended by good feelings alone. As he saw it, peace was not something that could be proclaimed by the victim, or the victim to be or the possible victim, but on the contrary, something that had to be collectively and rationally organized, structured, discussed, struggled for – even if this meant occasionally and provisionally resorting to defensive force. During the War of Independence, what he blamed the Philadelphia Quakers for was precisely the duplicity with which they brandished their principles in order, in fact, to leave a clear field for the troops of His Britannic Majesty, whom he then dubbed the '*Honorable* plunderer of his country' or the '*Right Honorable* murderer of mankind.'[65]

A few weeks after the Battle of Lexington, he launched his first attack on the Quakers, saying, 'I am thus far a Quaker, that I would gladly agree with all the world to lay aside the use of arms, and settle matters by negotiation; but unless the whole will, the matter ends, and I take up my musket and thank heaven he has put it in my power.'[66] This passage is well-known; less known but perhaps more precise and penetrating is the following one, taken from the same article (July 1775): 'The supposed quietude of a good man allures the ruffian ... The balance of power is the scale of peace. The same balance would be preserved were all the world destitute of arms, for all would be alike; but ... horrid mischief would ensure were one half of the world deprived of the use of them; for while avarice and ambition have a place in the heart of man, the weak will become a prey to the strong.'[67] Although he was later to dream of a military invasion of England, it is clear that, for Paine, only defensive wars were justifiable, and in his eyes such was the case of the American War: 'The period of debate is closed ... the appeal [to arms] was the choice of the king, and the continent has accepted the challenge.'[68] Hence his sarcastic remarks about the treacherous Society of Friends, whom he depicts as 'antiquated virgins ... mistaking [their] wrinkles for dimples'[69] and who, 'with the word "*peace, peace*" continually on their lips,' are so fond of supporting a government 'which is never better pleased than when at war!'[70] Paine could bite; but the Friends had a good memory and never forgave him, even on his deathbed.

One of Paine's most important contributions to the organization of peace was his *Maritime Compact* published in 1800. Written 'to compel the English government to acknowledge the rights of neutral commerce, and that free ships make free goods,'[71] this astonishing document, distributed to all foreign ministers then resident in Paris, was more generally designed to render war impossible by threatening belligerent nations with total commercial boycott on the part of neutral countries peacefully leagued into an 'Unarmed Association of Nations.'[72] The idea was that such a boycott would immediately ruin the aggressor's economy by cutting it off from the rest of the world, and thus render warfare counter-productive. The Association would have its own flag 'composed of the same colors as compose the rainbow'[73] and a presidency by rotation, 'the first president to be the executive power of the most northerly nation.'[74] In fact, Paine had in mind Paul I, Emperor of Russia, as the first possible president: 'had it not been for the untimely death of Paul,' he later contended, *'a law of Nations*, founded on the authority of nations ... would have been proclaimed.'[75]

This idea, and ideal, were not new for Paine. Eighteen years before, in his famous *Letter to the Abbé Raynal* (1782), he had already expressed similar views and summarized the whole issue with eloquence: 'The sea is the world's highway; and he who arrogates a prerogative over it transgresses the right [to the freedom of the ocean], and justly brings on himself the chastisement of nations.'[76] It was precisely in the same work – a reply to the Abbé's *Observations on the Revolution in America* – that, as an American historian has put it, he 'actually ceased to think in nationalistic terms and became a practical internationalist.'[77] Practical is perhaps not the right word, in the sense that Paine's utopian proposals were well ahead of his time and clearly overrated the degree of wisdom actually reached by his contemporaries. The novelties formulated in his *Letter* are well-known: the liberation of international trade, the organization of peace on a worldwide basis, a concerted limitation of armaments, and a federation of nations. Paine saw commerce as a convivial competition and as a means of international *rapprochement*. Hence his belief in the pacifying virtues of trade: 'Commerce,' he wrote, 'though in itself a moral nullity, has had a considerable influence in tempering the human mind.'[78] He also believed that, through the exemplary union of its thirteen states and its alliance with France, Spain, and the Netherlands, revolutionary America was in fact 'opening a new system of extended civilization'[79] and a new era during which the league of nations would at long last put an end to international violence and anarchy.

Less known, again, or less noticed, is the way in which Paine *first* insisted on the possibility of a peaceful entente between states with different political regimes, and *then* moved on to a conception of international progress that was much less ecumenical. When he wrote his *Letter to the Abbé Raynal*, Paine thought that nations could associate with each other in the name of peace and establish between themselves international rules independently of the nature of their several political regimes: 'Forms of government,' he insisted, 'have nothing to do with treaties.'[80] He had therefore no objection to a republic entering into an alliance with a monarchical country: 'So long as each performs its part, we have no more right or business to know how the one or the other conducts its domestic affairs.'[81] Although this may sound like Realpolitik, Paine's attitude was that of an idealist: 'It is best mankind should mix,' he went on to say, 'and it is by a free communication, without regard to domestic matters, that friendship is to be extended and prejudice destroyed all over the world,'[82] – prejudice which he so beautifully defined as 'the spider of the mind.'[83] But the most interesting argument here, and the most original, was Paine's presentation of the concert of nations as *a kind of international republic* where each member, regardless of its size or of the nature of its government, could have a say, and act as an equal partner, in the preparation of peace agreements. That all countries, 'be their forms what they may, are relatively republics with each other,' such was, he explained, 'the first and true principle of alliance.'[84]

Ten years later he had learned much and changed his mind in many ways. In the second part of *Rights of Man* (1792) he takes up again, and expands, the utopian themes outlined one decade before in his reply to Raynal, advocating this time: (1) a sort of *Alliance for Progress* in the form of a European Confederacy including England, France, and Holland; (2) a gradual but 'general dismantling of all the navies in Europe,' and (3) a joint pressure of the United States and Confederated Europe in order to obtain from Spain 'the independence of South America and the opening [of] those countries … to the general commerce of the world.'[85] But Paine was now convinced that his dream had no chance of coming true so long as England remained allergic to democratic and republican principles, so long as England remained a court government 'enveloped in intrigue and mystery,'[86] equally unable to cater for the actual needs of its people and to peacefully cooperate with such countries as had cast off the yoke of tyranny. He was confident that the establishment of a democratic system in Britain would powerfully contribute to the spread of republicanism throughout the world and to international peace.

The idea that British monarchy would be a perpetual cause of warfare became such an obsession with Paine that in 1796 he started contriving and planning a naval invasion of England, thus betraying his own previous attachment to the doctrine of defensive war. But, as he himself put it, it was still for the cause of *peace* that he was acting that way: 'The intention of the expedition [with Bonaparte appointed to the command] was to give the people of England an opportunity of forming a government for themselves, and thereby bring about peace.'[87] It happens that in the course of my research on Paine, I stumbled upon something which is to be found in none of the previous Tom Paine biographies: a classified report written *in French* by some secret agent then working in Paris for the English government. Dated 'January 1798,' the document explains that the French Directoire had drawn up a list of five British political personalities who were to form the English 'Directory' once the invasion was accomplished. And Paine was in the number, together with John Horne Tooke, William Sharp, John Thelwell, and the Marquis of Lansdowne![88] This secret scheme – and the prospect of having a share in one more revolution – may account for the fact that Paine lingered so many years in France after his release from prison.

Behind his dream of naval conquest lay the deeply-rooted creed that Britain's external violence was nothing but a projection of its own internal system based on social injustice, and that no lasting peace would be achieved in Europe while England remained the stronghold of hereditary inequality. More generally, Paine considered that the establishment of social peace in each and every civilized country was a prerequisite for a better understanding amongst the nations of the world. Hence his insistence, in *Rights of Man*, on the necessity of developing *social* as well as political rights, so as to diminish economic frustrations, bring men closer to one another, increase the amount of fraternity in the world, and diminish aggressive drives. For Paine, proposing 'plans for the education of helpless infancy, and the comfortable support of the aged and distressed'[89] was not only a just policy; it was also part of an active strategy of peace based on the idea that non-belligerence between nations does rest, to a not inconsiderable degree, on the establishment of social non-violence between the citizens of each national community.

Like all prophets, Paine was, so to speak, a 'delayed-fuse realist,' someone who had a clear view of the future at a time when so many minds were confused. He was not just the visionary of a more pacific future. He was an actor, a militant, and, if I may put it so, a 'soldier of peace.' He did not see world peace as merely a godsend resulting from chance of Providence, but as the reward of a long, patient, and difficult struggle. In other words, he was the reverse of a fatalist: 'Man,' he once wrote, 'must be the privy councillor of fate, or something is not right.'[90]

Clive Phillpot

In the Footsteps of Thomas Paine

It seems to me that my only justification for speaking today, since I have nothing new to add to the story of Thomas Paine, is that my own enthusiasm might perhaps be said to represent, idiosyncratically, some of the many Paine enthusiasts around the world who are not engaged in historical studies or research, but whose lives have been affected in some way by Paine's life, actions, or writings.

For a great many years my knowledge of Thomas Paine was limited to a perception of him as a figure of opposition in England, even a folk hero, mainly on account of his subversive writings, and his participation in the American and French Revolutions. Although his name was one to which I responded, this response had nothing to do with the history that I was taught at school. Indeed, when I began high school, in England, at the age of eleven, our class was taught history by the physical education instructor who had formerly served in the Navy. Our first year of history was confined exclusively to the life of Francis Drake, our second year solely to the life of Horatio Nelson. In the third year I learned something about the English three-field system, and then we dropped history permanently.

On reflection, I think that I first came across Paine's name in a Penguin paperback book on William Blake by Jacob Bronowski, and perhaps simultaneously in Blake's own verse, also in Penguin, notably in the revolutionary pantheon in his poem *America* that included: Washington, Franklin, Paine, and Warren; and at different times: Gates, Hancock, Green, Allen, and Lee.

The next occurrences of Paine's name that I remember were during the 1960s when I lived in Hastings in Sussex. This town has had a brief modern history, and is sometimes known as Mugsborough, which pseudonym was given to it in the pioneering Socialist novel, *The Ragged Trousered Philanthropists* [1914] by Robert Tressell. My discovery of this book, by friendship with the author's biographer, and the general political climate, led me to take a keen interest in the history of the common people in rural Sussex. In this way I became acquainted with the impact of Paine's *Rights of Man*, as well as becoming aware of his name, often in the company of William Cobbett, not to mention such characters as Captain Swing [fictional name of a rebel in the protests of impoverished farm workers across the agricultural south of England in 1830]. I also began taking library science at a London Polytechnic and here came across two books: [R. K.] Webb's *The British Working-Class Reader*, and [Richard] Altick's *The English Common Reader*, which I am sure mentioned Paine and his writings. I even began to read [Alfred Owen] Aldridge's biography of Paine, *Man of Passion*, but I did not get very far with it at the time.

I spent the next eight years working in London at the Chelsea School of Art, but my increasing involvement with art did not give Paine much of a look in. Then I was offered a job here in New York. The timing was perfect since I was feeling uncertain what my future might be in England. I arrived in New York in 1977. For a year or so I had a temporary work visa, and then finally got my 'green card,' otherwise known as my 'alien registration card.' Looking back I now realize that not only was I an alien, but I was also alien-ated from much that I found in the USA. The extent of this alienation was not really apparent to me at the time, and now I think that those people who listened to my criticisms of the USA were very forbearing in their response to the shallowness of my understanding of America. But I was serious about staying in the USA, for I had sold my house in England and brought my family with me. Indeed after a while I began to consider whether I should become an American citizen, instead of a permanent guest in the country. What I had difficulty with, however, was establishing roots, although hearing the statistic that 32% of Americans can trace their ancestry back to England, Scotland, or Wales gave me more of a feeling of kinship with Americans.

As a result of thinking about citizenship I read the United States Constitution and the Declaration of Independence, became interested in Jefferson's role in this process, and began to read histories: Nevins & Commager, Nye & Morpurgo's Pelican history, then Charles Beard, Edmund Morgan, and Eric Foner's *Tom Paine and Revolutionary America* – all paperbacks that I could pick up easily in new or secondhand bookstores.

From my reading I began to understand that America's independence from Britain was a very close-run thing, and that the recently-arrived Englishman, Thomas Paine, had a pivotal role in the decision to become independent. Eric Foner's book, in particular, also helped me to visualize Thomas Paine in Philadelphia, which by that time I knew quite well. I began to feel an empathy for Thomas Paine, especially with regard to his arriving in America from England and having to acclimatize himself to a somewhat different culture (and a different climate!), and at about the same age as myself when I arrived. I also developed immense respect for the fact that he became a major player on the stage of American history a mere fifteen months after he arrived in this country for the first time.

At about this time, several coincidences accelerated my interest in Thomas Paine. I saw a movie entitled *La Nuit de Varennes*, directed by Ettore Scola, which revolves around Louis XVI's flight from Paris in 1791, two years after the French Revolution. The director and his co-author invented a plot that could actually have taken place – though it did not, in fact – whereby the aging Casanova, representing the old world, played by Marcello Mastroianni, and Restif de la Bretonne, representing the revolutionary new world, played by Jean-Louis Barrault, find themselves chasing Louis XVI across France, accompanied by Thomas Paine, played by Harvey Keitel. The beauty of this near-factual fiction really intrigued me. Although Thomas Paine is a minor figure in the movie, the fact of his historical involvement in French affairs, as well as English and American, was brought home to me very forcibly.

Another event that drew me closer to Paine was that Penguin Books in the USA began to remainder their paperback copies of *Common Sense* and *Rights of Man*. Many of the bookstores that I visited in New York City seemed to have dozens of copies of those two books at less than a dollar each. Inevitably, I bought one of each for myself and began to taste Paine's distinctive prose, and relish his ideas expressed in his own words.

There was yet another coincidence. My brother and his wife and family have lived in different locations in Lincolnshire in England over the last decade. Several years ago they moved to Alford, a really beautiful small town, and inevitably I visited them there. On one visit my brother showed me a plaque on the side of the Windmill Hotel in the middle of his town that said that Thomas Paine had lived there from 1764 to 1765! But that was not all. When I was staying with my parents in Hurstpierpoint in Sussex, at about the same time, my father, responding to my enthusiasm for Paine, asked me if I realized that there was a house in the town of Lewes only eight miles away, in which Thomas Paine had lived in the 1770s! As you can imagine, these coincidences accelerated my interest in Thomas Paine still more. I now had a really personal involvement in his life story, and this led me to look for recently published biographies to discover more details of his life in England, and to see if my perception of him as a life-long radical was correct. Another thing that I did was to apply to join the Thomas Paine Society in England, and the Thomas Paine National Historical Association in the USA.

My interest in art and visual information caused me to be curious about Paine's features. The most ubiquitous image, to my mind deservedly so, was his friend William Sharp's engraving after Romney's 1792 portrait. But at the American National Portrait Gallery and at the Library of Congress, both in Washington, DC, I began to track down other images, including engravings after a lost portrait by Charles Willson Peale. It was there, too, that I saw for the first time the late-in-life oil painting of Paine, by another friend, John Wesley Jarvis.

Another visual aspect of Paine's life was his designs for bridges, and the bridge seemed to be a very appropriate symbol to be associated with him. I became eager to see the results of his visual imagination. Bridges and their builders had interested me for a long time, perhaps because of my own father's beginnings as an engineer, perhaps on account of a symbolic value that they had for me, certainly for their aesthetics. Recently, my father gave me his volumes of Samuel Smiles's *Lives of the Engineers*, which he had been given when an apprentice. The volume on roads and bridges, on Metcalfe and Telford, had an engraving of the iron bridge over the Wear River at Sunderland, said to have been derived at least in part from Paine's designs. (Recently, I went to see the iron bridge over the Wear.)

I think that I have talked enough about these coincidences, because in the end such coincidences are of no consequence if the figure to whom they refer is of no interest. Paine *was* of interest to me, and not just because I could use his odyssey as a way to create a meaningful place for myself in my new country, the United States. Although I had mixed feelings on leaving England in 1977, especially since my parents and my brother and his family were still there, I was not sorry to leave England during the ascendancy of Margaret Thatcher. The United States under Jimmy Carter seemed somewhat less reactionary than Britain would be under Thatcher. However, within a couple of years of my arrival in the

USA, Ronald Reagan was elected, and it became apparent that the Western world was undergoing a convulsion.

I do not mention the names of these two politicians to make a small point. In the early 1980s the swing to conservatism profoundly affected my personal optimism. For the first time in my thinking life, my belief in progress was very seriously dented. I could not believe that I was living in a time when so many prehistoric and reactionary ideas were given such currency, and in addition were unchallenged in the mainstream media. I was totally out of sympathy with the times. I began to understand that the notion of progress that I believed in had historical roots. My scientific education had also contributed to a belief in reason and logic, and in evolutionary progress. (As it happens, at the same time I was also experiencing a certain detachment from the more conspicuous varieties of contemporary art, which also seemed reactionary, and was seeking a more encompassing idea of what modernism might mean.)

All these factors led me back to the eighteenth century, and specifically to the Enlightenment. I had also, for many years, been very interested in such people as William Hogarth and Lawrence Sterne, the author of *The Life and Opinions of Tristram Shandy, Gentleman*, who in their respective spheres seemed to me to possesss 'modern' sensibilities. I began to make a deeper acquaintance of Voltaire and Diderot as thinkers and as writers; I began to take an interest in the history of science itself. It seemed to me that the eighteenth century not only marked a rupture with a past that I had difficulty in entering, but was also a period which seemed very accessible to me. One of the missing elements in the pantheon that I was making for myself, representing what I felt was the beginning of a kind of modernism, was a more purely political figure. It was here that Thomas Paine also fitted in. His contributions to the histories of two countries that underwent revolutions, and to the history of a third that suffered great strains but unfortunately did not undergo a revolution, seemed seminal. In addition, his ideas and writing struck some personal chord in me.

Thomas Paine became to me a true 'Founding Father' of the United States, and indeed of the modern world, to whom one could return in order to set one's compass through this time of reaction. Thomas Paine's clear expositions of his views: on the irrelevance of royalty and aristocracy; on the reactionary nature of organized religion; on the rights of all peoples, particularly as expressed through his attention to the rights of woman and the iniquity of slavery; on cooperation and coexistence between nations, but opposition to the tyranny of one nation over another; on the futility of war; on freedom of thought and freedom of speech; on the state's obligation to its weak and deprived citizens; and on many more matters, reflect his civilized attitudes and his continuing relevance. I sympathize with these essential ideas, and find myself drawn irresistibly to this rational man so uncommonly endowed with abundant common sense, and this citizen of the world.

Photographs by Clive Phillpot

Thetford: Thomas Paine Statue, King Street

Thetford: Thomas Paine Avenue

Thetford: Thomas Paine Hotel

Thetford: Thomas Paine Plaque

Alford: Windmill Hotel, Mamert Place

Alford: Paine Plaque at Windmill Hotel

Lewes: Bull House, Thomas Paine House

Lewes: Bull House, Thomas Paine Plaque

Lewes: White Hart Hotel

Lewes: White Hart Hotel Paine Plaque

Paul O'Dwyer

Thomas Paine Never Died

Friends and Admirers of Tom Paine,

First, let me compliment Leo W. Zonneveld of United Teilhard Trust on his initiative in provoking international interest in Thomas Paine in a United Nations setting. It is most appropriate that a discussion of Paine's life be held on the premises of an institution similar to one which he advocated nearly one hundred and seventy years before it became a reality.

Recently, the National Emergency Civil Liberties Committee presented me with the Thomas Paine Award. A friend of mine, a member of the Awards Committee, in a test of modesty, asked if I really believed I deserved it. I said that if the criterion was a deep commitment to the principles annunciated by Paine, I felt sure there were thousands of Paine admirers throughout the world who might be more deserving of the honor, but I felt if the coveted award was to be presented to the person whose quiet life was most rattled by the accounts of Tom Paine's life and whose mind was most disrupted by Paine's writings, I consider that I would have a fair chance of leading the pack.

I came here from Ireland at the age of seventeen and a half, having already lived through the most recent Irish Rebellion, also known then as the Black and Tan War and carelessly referred to nowadays in Dublin as the 'War of Independence,' which left the country half free and all slave with Lincoln's assessment of the ultimate effect such a state of affairs at least partially borne out. The end of that conflict left me and other young people like me disappointed, frustrated, and embittered, and I felt betrayed as I left for the new land I knew little about. Furthermore, being too preoccupied by the recent Irish Rebellion, I was only dimly aware that there were then other armed struggles for freedom coming to a boil in other areas in the world. I knew little about the American Revolution, and I had never heard of Thomas Paine.

This was the state of my mind when my ship, the *Doric* of the White Star line, pulled into New York Harbor with its 'tempest tossed' cargo anxious to get inside 'The Golden Door.' New York and its bustle does not permit its citizens to wallow in self-pity, and soon the memory, the long frustrating struggle for freedom, was replaced with personal ambition and a kindling hope of a better life with security and the acknowledgement that here an immigrant, particularly an Irish immigrant, could make it and make it well. This immigrant found himself without effort to have the advantage over native-born American Negroes, Jews, Slavs, and Italians, but that was the way it was in America, and since it favored me, I found no fault with the system. Long gone and long forgotten were the signs 'No Irish Need Apply,' and if the sentiment was applied to others, that was no skin off this Irish nose. Within the year I had finished my pre-law courses at Fordham University and was working on the waterfront in a union job and ready to pursue fame and fortune because that's what I felt one should do to be a good citizen of my new country. The system of poverty which afflicted Southern and Appalachian whites and the evaluation of the black population by their white fellow citizens everywhere gave me no qualms. I did get a temporary jolt when Professor O'Connor of Fordham told our class what a wonderful world it would be if the Catholic Church were the temporal as well as spiritual ruler of the universe. I had some experience with the role of the Church in Ireland. Its hierarchy had come out squarely and vigorously and with all its power on the side of Empire during every bid for freedom that took place during the previous century. This lecture was delivered in the Woolworth Building about the time the Democratic Party was preparing to offer Al Smith as their candidate for President of the United States.

Anyway, it did not occur to me that there was a basic inconsistency in a 'democratic' society which for a century and a half had preached equality and had simultaneously practiced rank discrimination and outright bigotry. If I thought at all, it was that an immigrant must be grateful for his blessings and that should be translated into fighting for his new country in time of distress and following the flag, joining the parade, and shouting for America. That was 1926 and, with homesickness on the wane, the world seemed bright and I felt no urge to rock the boat. But in the history class I learned that slavery had existed in each of the British colonies and even the rebellious colonists held on to the degrading system even as the revered Declaration of Independence proclaimed that all men were created equal. Then, I don't know who (he may have been a fellow scholar or it may have been my brother Bill) gave me *The Age of Reason* and *Rights of Man*, and the placid acceptance of the status quo, contentment and peace of mind went out of my life forever. The windows of my mind flew open, which provided me with a new insight, clarified some muddled thinking which previously had held me ignorant and confused. I took to reading other Paine writings and after a while a new biography by Howard Fast and another one by a man named [W. E.] Woodward, who challenged some of Fast's contentions, and in the course of time other writers. As I read these volumes the words jumped out of the pages, challenging my most profound beliefs.

They jolted me out and away from the placid, comfortable life into which I was heading with all that it entailed. I know that traveling along the old route I would have joined the right clubs and would have accepted without question the wisdom of my elders who had already arrived or who were on their way up the political and financial ladders. More frequently now back into my mind came the harrowing memory of an alien savage army ruthlessly demonstrating its power over me and my neighbors and my country, except that now I was coming to the realization that the battle must be carried on in a thousand fronts. I now was aware that the disease was worldwide and it infected every corner of my new country, and my respect and admiration for Paine grew as I realized he conducted a lonely fight against slavery and risked his life in France as he opposed capital punishment as Louis faced the guillotine. In the course of time I concluded I could no longer follow Stephen Decatur [American naval officer and hero in Barbary Wars and War of 1812] even as I knew that expressing such an attitude would bring into question my loyalty to America and was likely to brand me unfaithful and ungrateful. But Paine made it clear what course I had to follow and a real emancipation of the soul had begun, and I was henceforth to march to a new drum and to quote another hero, 'damn the consequences.' Now there was no turning back.

So I found myself examining the 'truths' that I had previously accepted without question, and as time progressed from there on to the battle to contain the forces of the House Committee on Un-American Activities. As a lawyer I knew that the A.B.A. [American Bar Association] was a powerful institution totally opposed to progress, so I joined and was promoted to the leadership of the new liberal National Lawyers Guild. That brought no well-heeled clients to my door, and I charged that Tom Paine has been totally responsible for the destruction of my plan to seek an appointment to the prosecutor's office with all the promise it held for me, and to march me instead into a political career of a different sort which seldom got me public approval. Whenever I faltered or was tempted by the fleshpots, there was Paine on my shoulder crying shame.

So I went to Russia when *Glastnost* was not even a dream, and to Spain in the last days of Franco, and I joined the International Association of Democratic Lawyers and fought the House Committee and the oppressive laws like literacy tests for voting, and it was Paine who drove me to Hazard, Kentucky with Phil Sipser [labor lawyer and political activist] to battle on the Federal Courts for fair play for striking coal miners, and to Mississippi to join in the battle for civil and voting rights, and in Northern Ireland where the British courts had turned their backs on the *Magna Carta* and rejected the jury system which they proudly boasted they had initiated, and to London to bear witness to the Birmingham Six travesty.

The problems created by my acquaintanceship with Tom Paine really crested when I got to City Hall after being elected President of the New York City Council. I thought that my election provided me with a good opportunity to create some sort of memorial someplace in the City and State in which he lived and died – a marker that would commemorate the contribution that this magnificent world patriot had made to the City of New York and to the United States of America and incidentally to Ireland in 1798.

The response to my proposal left me with the conviction that Tom Paine had not really died. The experience reminded me of Joe Hill, who lost his life in the struggle for decency in the working place, and the song set to his memory:

> I dreamt I saw Joe Hill last night
> As plain, as plain could be
> I said, 'Joe Hill, you're ten years dead'
> 'I never died,' said he.

And I thought of President Theodore Roosevelt who never read Paine but who dubbed him 'a filthy little atheist.'

I attempted to get the West Side Highway called after Paine. Under some rules, which I regret to say I was a sponsor, such a proposal had to go before the regional planning boards along that road. One of the regions included Bohemia in Greenwich Village where Paine died. The area now encompasses the homes of artists, writers, and liberals. I thought in this environment my idea would gain enthusiastic approval. To my amazement, even there the burghers rejected the concept, assuring me, however, that their rejection was not to be construed as a lack of devotion to Paine, but they felt someplace other than the highway which passed their doors would be more appropriate. In the Civil Rights movement we had become accustomed to that reaction, but usually it occurred in middle or upper class sections. Nothing daunted, I tried another Manhattan area. I heard that there was a small park around the swank Plaza Hotel which had not been given a name. I presented my proposal to two local planning boards in that region – one in the silk stocking district and one closely associated with it. Both objected to the idea, and the park remains orphaned to this day with nothing there to claim association with our country's past. Later on I was explaining my predicament to Henry Steele Commager and to my amazement that legendary figure disapproved totally of my most recent effort. 'Tom Paine,' he said, 'would revolt at the idea of being in any way associated with the Plaza.'

In my frustration with New York's bureaucrats, I found myself confiding in a compatriot who like myself is an amateur historian. I explained my predicament to him. He was and is associated with the Parks Department and perforce he shall be nameless. He promised to help, and to whet his appetite I told him of a discovery Linda Fisher, another Paine admirer, who did public relations work for me at City Hall, had made. During the Bicentennial she dug out from the New York Historical Society some long forgotten Paine writings. They contained a letter which Paine had written to [Robert] Livingston pleading for mercy for a man named James Napper Tandy. That opened up another chapter in the life of Paine. It was said that the cock that crowed in America awakened the people of France. It also beckoned the Irish Presbyterians and dissenters who fought valiantly against Britain and for the freedom of Ireland in the Rebellion of the United Irishmen in 1798. In Paris, Paine and the Irish Revolutionaries met frequently and a friendship developed between them. Wolfe Tone, the Rebellion's leader, complained that Napper Tandy and Paine were spending too much time in the Grog House, and the cause of freedom had suffered. Later, Napper Tandy who was captured in Hamburg, and to Napoleon's chagrin, was handed over to the British. Livingston responded to Paine and saved Napper Tandy from being transported.

But that's a whole other story. So, my friendly informant came through with the discovery that there was a spot in the oldest part of the City still unnamed. And so Thomas Paine Park was born, and I invited the City fathers and the council members to be there to share in the dedication. It was a dry day and a fine day. Many of Paine's admirers were there, but of the City fathers only W. Bernard Richland, a native of Liverpool and the City's most erudite Corporation Counsel ever, was the one City official to appear at the ceremonies. So, there it is – a square block with benches and trees and grass – and it is officially dedicated to the memory of one of the world's most profound thinkers to whom all Americans now, in the past and as long as this Republic stands, owe an everlasting debt of gratitude.

Six months ago (June 18, 1987), four thousand New Yorkers, dedicated to the protection of our rights, demonstrated in Thomas Paine Park across the street from the Prosecutor's office, the Federal Courts, and the Federal Correctional Institution, where Joe Doherty, who never offended the laws of the United States in any way, has been held without bail for five long years pending deportation to Northern Ireland, and the name Tom Paine was invoked by the speakers and the press, and I now believe that master historian, Henry Steele Commager, was right. Tom Paine will live forever, facing the Department of Justice and the Federal Prison to remind prosecutors and to remind the judges who there preside that there once was a revolution here and that our forebears did make a big point of enacting a Bill of Rights. I was there on the speaker's platform because Tom Paine was on my shoulders urging me on. Since the day sixty years ago when I became acquainted with him in the pages of his writings he has never let me alone. It was for that reason that facetiously I told my friend in the N.E.L.C. that the trouble Mr. Paine has caused me throughout my adult life makes me eligible above all others for their prized award.

Sean Wilentz

Paine's Legacy

In his lifetime, Thomas Paine heard his praises sung on two continents. Literally *sung*:

> There was a man whose name was Paine, a man of Common Sense,
> Who came from Philadelphia, his knowledge to dispense,
> He prov'd that man had equal rights, as equal sons of nature,
> Deriv'd by universal grant, from Heaven's Legislature.

So ran a London song from 1794. No one, so far as I know, has collected all of the Paineite songs from the late eighteenth century, but their number must run into the dozens. The most famous of them, Joseph Mather's 'God Save Great Thomas Paine,' was sung to the tune of both 'God Save the King' and 'My Country 'Tis of Thee' – a fitting tribute (as Christopher Hitchens has observed) to a man who was both the founding father of modern British radicalism and the finest American. Few of these songs are sung today, especially in America (although there is a popular fiddle tune, 'The Rights of Man,' that is still recorded from time to time). More important, relatively few people really know much about the best-selling author of the Age of Revolution. Has Paine's legacy, like his bones, been lost along the way?

Yes and no. There are at least some monuments to Paine's memory. In the towns of Thetford and Lewes, England, and in New Rochelle, New York, stalwart bands of Paine admirers – freethinkers, labor activists, and history buffs and others – have been kindling Paine's legacy for years. Twelve years ago, the City of New York had set aside a patch of land near Foley Square as Thomas Paine Park. But for the most part, existing national governments have shied away from commemorating Paine, aside from the odd plaque or postage stamp, which is hardly adequate. These honors are usually reserved for heads of state, but how, then, are we to explain the popularity of Ben Franklin or Robert Fulton, let alone the endless procession of minor military heroes and party hacks and the neglect of Thomas Paine? The oversight is scandalous, but also understandable. Paine, the international democrat, put little stock in the kinds of unreflective patriotic nationalism usually invested in alabaster national heroes. And Paine's writings, with their insistence on speaking plain truth to insolent power, still have a way of unsettling the powers that be, two centuries later.

Given the dearth of official glory, we must look a little harder to find Paine's legacy. Abstractly, Paine is certainly remembered in his dedication to reason, and his name is linked to two cardinal principles of modern political life – democracy and internationalism. Getting beneath these abstractions turns up some interesting things about how Paine, the citizen of the world, is remembered – and not remembered – around the world. Paine's exploits touched most directly the experiences of three nations: France, Great Britain, and the United States. He is honored today in all three, but in very different ways.

France seems to have done the least to preserve a Paineite tradition (despite the fine efforts of contemporary scholars like Bernard Vincent). It is not entirely a matter of xenophobia or French national pride. (After all, President Wilson has his avenue in Paris.) It was, instead, the French Revolution – or more specifically the Jacobin ascendency – that undid Paine in France. Ensconced in Paris in 1792, an official American representative to the French Convention, Paine was one of the best friends the French Revolution would ever have, more eloquent in its defense than most of the French revolutionaries themselves. But for various reasons – linguistic, temperamental, intellectual, accidental – Paine drifted into the milieu of the emerging Girondin faction. Once he raised his voice in 1793 against the execution of Louis XVI (on both humanitarian and pragmatic grounds), Paine's political position became, to put it mildly, precarious. He paid for his alleged unreliability to the revolutionary cause with ten months in a Jacobin prison.

It is misleading to see in Paine's French experience (as some writers have) a kind of foreshadowing of twentieth-century political agonies – of liberators turned into jailers and naïve radicals turned into victims, and others into bitter conservatives. Such a picture seems to me designed more to gain some ideological advantage than to reason with the past. Paine was never naïve; more important, even after his release from prison, he never renounced his support for the French Revolution. Indeed, he continued to take pride at the thought that the American struggle for independence and his own writings may have helped inspire the French to overturn the Bastille. But to the extent that Jacobinism has become all too synonymous with the revolutionary cause, then it is easy to see why Paine's role in the French Revolution has been all but forgotten. Girondist politics are today largely consigned to history's dustbin, as is anyone even fleetingly associated with that point of view.

When recalled, Paine's *Rights of Man* is commonly described as part of a debate over British government (which in part, of course, it was). Paine's actual contribution to French developments – as well as any larger Paineite tradition in France – has gotten lost in the folds of French politics, amidst the competing claims of those neo-Jacobin republicans, socialists, Bonapartists, and conservatives who have dominated French politics and, in effect, re-fought the French Revolution for generation after generation. Even today, as some French intellectuals and politicians try to retrieve a viable Gallic liberalism, their thoughts turn not to Thomas Paine but to a writer like Aléxis de Tocqueville or like [François] Guizot.

Paine's reputation is far sturdier in Britain. Literary background is one reason why: Paine's writing is above all in the great tradition of the freeborn, dissenting English democrat, a tradition with its roots in Bunyan, Milton, and the russet-coated writers of the Commonwealth period. As various historians have shown, that tradition fed directly into the culture and politics of the nineteenth-century British labor movement, with Tom Paine's writings as its foundation texts. Ever since, Paine's memory has burned strongest in the British labor movement, and more recently: the Labour Party. Other legacies – of John Wesley and of Karl Marx – are there as well. Still, there is a fairly direct line leading from Paine to the Chartists who held Paine's writings aloft, and then to the later generations of trade unionists and socialists and activists who sing to this day about the rights of man – including Michael Foot, M.P., Labour Party Leader, and President of the Thomas Paine Society.

The United States is a more puzzling case. Here, the praise of Paine began to abate in the late 1790s, not because of his Girondist sympathies but because of his anti-Christian deism. Americans could easily celebrate Paine for *Rights of Man*; they could not forgive him *The Age of Reason*, not at a time when a fervent evangelical revival was gearing up, a revival that would usher in an American nineteenth century marked by intense piety. In 1809, Paine's former friend Joel Barlow advised the New York City editor James Cheethan that 'the greater part of the readers in the United States will not be persuaded, as long as their present feelings last, to consider Paine in another light than as a drunkard and a deist.'

Cheetham proved Barlow correct a year later when he published his notorious biography, which did so much to codify the Paine demonology. From that day to this, America's national political leaders have usually had precious little to say about Paine and his works – at least in public. Thomas Jefferson (who, it should be recalled, was a slaveholder) has become the mainstream apostle of reason, enlightenment, and equality. The most pungent remark from a nineteenth-century or early twentieth-century American president about Paine was Theodore Roosevelt's absurd dismissal of him as a 'filthy little atheist.' In the twentieth century, since then (and some may view this as ironic), it has taken Ronald Reagan to do the most to cite Paine approvingly – the conservative president who takes courage from Paine's radical call to remake the world.

Yet just beneath the surface a stronger American Paineite political tradition has ebbed and flowed. Despite the notoriety attached to his name in some quarters, Paine's contributions to the language of American politics, and to Americans' sense of what it means to be an American, were too fundamental to let his ideas suffer utter neglect. Andrew Jackson, a firm proponent of the separation of church and state as well as of other democratic principles, once allowed that Paine should be honored 'in the hearts of all lovers of liberty.' Abraham Lincoln, likewise, admired Paine, particularly for his religious skepticism. Outside of the American political mainstream, the Paineite current has run even stronger. On January 29, 1825, a group of some forty radical artisan freethinkers (some of them English immigrants), all of them drawn from roughly the same local strata that so thrilled Paine during the American Revolution, gathered in New York City to honor Paine's birthday. They began a tradition of annual celebrations that expanded and spread through the 1840s, encompassing a significant portion of the Jacksonian labor movement. At roughly the same time, partisans of the radical wing of the Democratic Party honored Paine and spoke continually on the stump about Paineite principles. One of their number, the great sculptor John Frazee, actually designed and executed a handsome monument to the author of *Common Sense.*

Other voices, usually voices of dissent, perpetuated the Paineite tradition after the Civil War. The ex-artisan poet of democracy, Walt Whitman, saw fit to address a Paine birthday celebration in 1877, where he proclaimed that a good portion of what was best about his country –

'its ardent belief in, and substantial practice of, radical human rights' – derived from Thomas Paine. Later Americans, less sure that the country was still in touch with its highest ideals, turned to Paine for sustenance. Eugene V. Debs often made a point of insisting that the American socialist tradition owed much to Paine. When the National Association for the Advancement of Colored People founded its newspaper early in this century, it could find no better title than *The Crisis*. And on through the 1960s, American reformers and radicals of various stripes paid homage to Paine, occasionally in a calculated search for legitimacy, more often not.

Taken country by country, then, Paine's legacy is uneven. Still, a common thread runs through these different examples – of Paine as the hero of democratic causes not yet won and of causes sometimes forgotten, the prophet who was honored and then dishonored in his own time and whose main legacy is to the powerless. There is much truth in this, but it is not the whole story. Viewing Paine as a visionary utopian tells us much about how the world has departed from what Paine considered to be self-evident natural principles – but it also obscures that side of Paine that was eminently practical. It is to forget the Paine who spent countless hours computing the actual economic costs of monarchical corruption. It is to forget the Paine who worked tirelessly as the clerk of the Pennsylvania assembly, helping to hammer out the state's first emancipation law. It is to forget the Paine who designed iron bridges, smokeless candles, and countless other scientific improvements. It is to forget the projects of Paine's that did come to pass.

As a writer, for example, Paine established a style, mixing plainspoken politics with seditious laughter, which has become a mainstay of public criticism. He was, in effect, one of the first, if not the first, of the modern political intellectuals. Earlier writers, to be sure, had spoken eloquently of the people and to the people, as [John] Bunyan and [Gerrard] Winstanley did. Aspects of Paine's writings are heavily indebted to writers like [Jonathan] Swift, to say nothing of the more malicious and salacious pamphleteers of eighteenth-century Grub Street. But it was Paine who most forcefully directed his talents to the crises of the moment, in a compelling language designed to galvanize not so much the people in and around the Court or the capital but those ordinary people whose reading consisted mainly of the Bible (if that) – an everyday language drawn from the pulpit and the State House but also from the tavern, the workshop, the kitchen, and the streets. It is impossible to imagine a Mark Twain, a Henry George, or an H. L. Mencken, without Tom Paine in back of them all. Here Paine's practical project became a living reality. The same is true of numerous other of Paine's efforts, from the very independence of the American republic to such later developments as the abolition of slavery and the founding of the United Nations. We fail to notice this side of Paine's legacy, not because it is hidden or because it has not come to pass, but because it is everywhere.

Where, then, between Paine the visionary and Paine the practical man, are we to locate Paine's legacy? It is, I think, in the tension between the two – the unfulfilled visions and the living realities – that his writings still contain their great power. This is not always self-evident, either to historians, politicians, or citizens. To them, too often, Paine's writings may be inspiring on the subjects of democracy and internationalism, but they also seem to be based on an obsolete view of the world. All of Paine's rationalist talk about natural laws, human benevolence, and universal rights does grate somewhat on twentieth-century ears. We have learned too much about the potentialities of human evil and irrationality – from Auschwitz to the Gulag to everyday conflicts of class, race, and nationality – to be as optimistic about humankind as Paine was. Paine's democracy, some say, was a patently 'bourgeois' democracy, a forerunner of the individualist ideals that would eventually be used to mask the wretched exploitation of mine and mill. Paine's democracy, others insist, is unrealistic in today's treacherous world; instead, we need secret governments of unelected spooks, soldiers, and crooks to keep the world safe from tyranny. As for internationalism, it is a nice idea, and worth trying sometime – but national security comes first.

Such people should be careful about condescending to Thomas Paine. We may feel uncomfortable with the scientistic optimism of democracy with which Paine viewed humanity. But to equate Paine's vision of democracy – or democracy itself – with human oppression is to make a mockery of *Common Sense*. Likewise the claim that to protect democracy, governments must circumvent the popular will. Were Paine alive today listening to his modern critics, I am sure he would be scribbling away somewhere, cackling to himself, telling us in no uncertain terms that we have not yet begun even to imagine what democracy could be like. The principles, even some of the institutions of democracy are here; practical Tom Paine helped put them in place two centuries ago. But we have only begun to put them to the full use Paine thought possible.

The same holds true on the international scene. Slowly, painfully, and only at the cost of appalling carnage has the world slowly awakened to the imperative of international accord, and to the essential meaninglessness of the conventional nationalist wisdom. Even the threat of nuclear annihilation has not done the trick, for it has taken forty years and more of Cold War and continual crises for the living generations to begin to discard their shibboleths and begin to think – really think – about cooperation. There are, as I speak, fragile but not imaginary hopes that some fundamental change in human consciousness is underway. We will be sure this is so when governments start heeding the governed instead of the imperatives of national security – when throughout the world people appreciate Thomas Paine and understand as he did that the fate of democracy and the fate of human existence are as one. As Paine wrote in *Rights of Man*:

> That there are men in all countries who get their living by war, and by keeping up the quarrels of Nations, is as shocking as it is true; but when those who are concerned in the government of a country, make it their study to sow discord, and cultivate prejudices between Nations, it becomes the more unpardonable.

Only democracy – true democracy – could, as Paine saw it, rid the nations of the world of those who get their living by war, by sowing discord, and cultivating prejudice. Human conflict and evil will never be eliminated from the world. But we have it in our power, as practical utopians, to do far better than ever before. Let that, above all, be Paine's legacy.

David Henley

Thomas Paine: An Emerging Portrait

Tom Paine practically started this whole country.
Billie in Garson Kanin's *Born Yesterday*

With Thomas Paine it's all or nothing – there's very little middle ground. As we have repeatedly heard in this Colloquium, his unparalleled advocacy of the universal democratic/republican principles of self-determination and freedom gave rise to the establishment of the U.S. and the U.N.; yet, as we have often been reminded, he is virtually overlooked in connection with both. Indeed, this is the very first scholarly conference that I am aware of that is solely devoted to the subject of Thomas Paine; that this unprecedented and historical event is finally taking place right here in the world's top political forum is perfectly illustrative of my point. So be it. This lofty level of inquiry is, in my opinion, commensurate with the importance of the subject. To the sponsors, organizers, and participants go the honor, enlightenment, and joy of being the first to gather in this manner of scholarly acclaim of our most cherished founder. It is better to start at the top than not at all. Isn't this the way of the visionary?

My purpose here is to focus upon this anomalous treatment of Thomas Paine by briefly reviewing some of his more notable achievements that are not always fully recognized, and, at the same time, identifying (and complaining of) some of the more flagrant abuses. This inconsistent historical portrait of Paine will be considered in the framework of three pictorial dimensions: (1) a *self-portrait* as drawn by the man himself, by the imprint of his direct involvement in the momentous events of his day, and by the effect of his writings with pen and ink on paper (fortunately, acid-free at the time thus virtually indestructible); (2) a *historical portrait* painted over time by others such as biographers and historians, admirers and detractors; and (3) three actual *artistic portraits* rendered in oil on canvas (or engravings) by master portrait artists of the late eighteenth century.

Regardless of general neglect, Thomas Paine has been recognized by devotees as deserving credit for more notable and diverse achievements than any other person of his era. We are well aware that:

- He was the first to publicly, unequivocally, and effectively denounce chattel slavery in America;

- He was the first to propose and implement through brilliant persuasion *both* our independence from England and our representative form of government;
- He was the first to call for a constitutional convention and supply an outline for our constitution;
- He coined the term 'United States of America';
- He nurtured the Revolution through immortal words and practical deeds such as initiating the first fund-drive for the war effort, which resulted in his being the first subscriber to the Bank of North America, and he secured finances from France for the decisive battle of Yorktown;
- He was among the first to express concern for animal rights and nature;
- He was the first to delineate the social welfare system we take for granted today;
- He carried the American Revolution to Europe, resulting in the democratic movement of the late eighteenth and nineteenth centuries which ultimately led to the Third World Revolution of the twentieth;
- He was the first to publicly call for the overthrow of the French monarchy and wrote the French Declaration of Rights;
- He was the first to propose an international peace organization;
- He was the first to propose international arbitration and copyright;
- He founded the world's first Deistic Church which formed the basis for contemporary Humanist-Ethical-Unitarian movements;
- He pioneered the development of the metal arch-bridge, the steam boat, and the internal combustion engine;
- He was the first to propose the development of the Northwest Territories and purchase of the Louisiana Territory;
- In terms of per capita readership at the time of publication, he wrote four of the greatest selling books in the history of writing: *Common Sense*, *American Crisis*, *Rights of Man*, and *The Age of Reason* – no political writer of the eighteenth century has more books still in print.

One must admit, however, that in spite of the above record of achievement, only *Common Sense* receives any degree of recognition today in our history books, and this only sparingly and begrudgingly. In reviewing the typical chapter dealing with that glorious year of 1776, it is notable that the chronology of events almost always begins with the publication of *Common Sense*; and *Common Sense* is almost always the last notable utterance mentioned as having occurred directly prior to the writing of the Declaration of Independence. The typical American History under consideration usually glosses over this interconnected chain of events in two or three paragraphs (rarely exceeding a page), while including a brief (but inspiring) quote or two, together with no significant background and discernable future. A few of the more enlightened historians will add that as he was the one that commenced the hostilities of 1776, with *Common Sense* in January, he was also the one to end the year in December by supplying both the motto and much needed reassurance for the Revolution in his immortal opening lines of the *American Crisis*, 'These are the times that try men's souls.' Washington, seeking a battle cry and backbone for his deserting army, recognized that both had arrived in the nick of time, supplied by Paine's pen. Washington then mustered his entire army to stand at attention for the first military inoculation on record, by having read to them the entire magnificent text (and some say he included *Common Sense* in the dissertation). It must have worked, for coincidence or not, the first victory was won immediately thereafter, to close out the year in question.

Paine's blazing self portrait became as clear as the words that spoke for themselves. In going on to consider the historical portrait as painted by others, I would like to focus particularly on Paine's stature as it emerged from his writings of 1776, because this was the period that basically determined his rightful claim as co-founder of the nation. A few thematic quotes by several notable admiring historians and biographers concerning the impact of *Common Sense* may serve to reinforce for us the emerging historical portrait we see today. A thousand words, in this case, are worth one indelible *historical picture*:

Table I. Quotes from historians on the effects of *Common Sense* on American Independence

It came from the press in Philadelphia early in January, 1776, the year the Congress uttered its Declaration of Independence. It was hard to resist its quick, incisive sentences, which cut so unhesitatingly to the heart of every matter they touched; which spoke, not the arguments of the lawyer, and were as direct and vivid in their appeal as any sentences of Mr. Swift himself could have been. They were cast, every one, not according to the canons of taste, but according to the cannons of force, and declared, every one, without qualification, for independence. Upon that, the issue was joined.[91]

With the publication of *Common Sense* in January, 1776, Thomas Paine broke the ice that was slowly congealing the revolutionary movement.[92]

Thomas Paine's famous pamphlet, *Common Sense*, convinced thousands of Americans that reconciliation was a dream and independence was a practical necessity. Thus was the spirit of independence unleashed.[93]

In January, there appeared in Philadelphia a pamphlet by Thomas Paine entitled *Common Sense*, which was to sell by the hundred thousands and to do more than any other utterance to turn the tide definitely toward independence.[94]

In by far the most famous publication of the time, *Common Sense*, it was urged that nothing short of a continental government could insure domestic peace; and this publication was endorsed by zealous Whigs from Massachusetts to Carolina.[95]

There was no doubt the business was progressing. Yet, the people continued hesitant, fearful. The radical leaders themselves were not fully aware of what it was that kept the body of their supporters from coming out openly for independence. To perceive it, interpret it, above all to give it voice, required not a statesman but an artist. And in the very nick of time, the very hour and second of indecision, the artist appeared.[96]

His book was to the American Revolution what *Uncle Tom's Cabin* was to the Civil War ... The value of Paine's book to the Revolutionary cause was enormous. It was a crystallizer, everything it said was already floating around nebulously, and without center of gravity, in the American mind; *Common Sense* brought the whole galaxy of revolutionary ideas into coherent form.[97]

... Paine's services to the Revolution were beyond calculation.[98]

Table II. Quotes from biographers on the effects of *Common Sense* on American Independence

Paine was the man who started the American Revolution, by his pamphlet *Common Sense*.[99]

It supplied the common people with reasons, and gave statesmen arguments.[100]

... the influence and power of this fifty-page pamphlet can hardly be exaggerated.[101]

The publication of *Common Sense* was like the breaking of a dam which releases all the pent-up water that stood behind it.[102]

It was the first argument for separation, the first assault upon the British *form* of government, the first blow for a republic, and it aroused our fathers like a trumpet's blast ... No other pamphlet ever accomplished such wonderful results ... Everywhere the people responded, and in a few months the Continental Congress declared the colonies free and independent states ... It is simple justice to say that Paine did more to cause the Declaration of Independence than any other man.[103]

Paine's 'Common Sense' prepared the public's mind for Independence and presented some of the outstanding reasons which were embodied in the Declaration of Independence, which was adopted six months thereafter.[104]

That the fourth of July, 1776, would not have witnessed the Declaration of Independence but for the timely appearance of 'Common Sense,' no candid, impartial student of history would for a moment question.[105]

Important as were some of Paine's mechanical inventions, they seem to me of minor interest, however, when we consider Paine's planning of this great American republic, of which he may very justly be termed the real founder.[106]

I have already noted the causal relationship between *Common Sense* and the Declaration of Independence. Several of the above quotes bear witness to the inseparability of the two. I have not the space here to support in depth the claim of Paine's actual authorship of the original Declaration. Sufficient for the purpose of this paper on oversights is to point out that there is a large and compelling literature relating to the subject and that this available published evidence is being systematically ignored. Aside from the merits of the case, the refusal of almost all contemporary Paine biographers to even indicate in their bibliographies that there are several serious studies which conclusively confirm Paine's authorship, is the most blatant example of continuing neglect that I know of relating to Paine scholarship.

Personally, it makes me feel better to know and espouse that a non-slaveholder and a somewhat more enthusiastic patriot wrote the founding document of this nation.

Believe me, dear sir, there is not in the British empire a man who more cordially loves a union with Great Britain than I do.[107]

Compare that quote from Thomas Jefferson with Paine's summation from *Common Sense*:

… nothing can settle our affairs so expeditiously as an open and determined DECLARATION OF INDEPENDENCE.[108]

Please note that both of the above statements were written at approximately *the same time*. Not that Jefferson could not have changed his mind. Indeed, his position on the necessity of separation changed quickly and radically, in all likelihood, as with all of the other founders, with an irresistible assist from *Common Sense*. It is understandable that Jefferson scholars avoid the controversy over the original authorship like the plague, for it is an embarrassment to them. (Not one Jefferson biography, or specific history of the writing of the Declaration of Independence, attempts to refute the arguments supporting Paine's authorship; in fact, they usually ignore him all together.) Paine biographers, likewise, either totally ignore the subject or merely make a weak point that Paine is only tangentially associated with the Declaration. So be it. If they are afraid to confront the issue or think that it does Paine no good from a historical perspective, they should at least reference the relevant literature in their bibliographies so that readers are aware of the controversy and can make up their own minds as to the merits and importance of the case.

The above quote from *Common Sense* at least shows that to Paine goes the honor of being the very first person to actually *write* the words 'DECLARATION OF INDEPENDENCE.' The following works present the case that he first wrote more than the title:

Table III. Works supporting Paine's authorship of First Draft of Declaration of Independence

- *Junius Unmasked; and Thomas Paine Author of the Declaration of Independence*, Joel Moody, 1874.

- *Modern Thinkers*, Van Buren Denslow, 1880.
- *Who Wrote the Declaration of Independence?* Wm. M. Van der Weyde, 1925.
- *Thomas Paine, Author of the Declaration of Independence*, Joseph Lewis, 1947.
- *Mysteries of History, No. 33, Who Wrote the Declaration of Independence?* Albert Payson Terhune, 1928.

All of the books listed above, with the exception of Joseph Lewis's, are very scarce and can be found only in rare book libraries, or Thomas Paine archives such as the American Philosophical Society Library in Philadelphia, and the Thomas Paine National Historical Association Library in New Rochelle. The above work by William M. Van der Weyde, the Association's long-time president, shows that the question of Paine's authorship was of great import to the members in the 1920s. Oh, were it so today!

The lesser known, but equally important, question concerning Paine's unattributed writings revolves around the mysterious Letters of Junius. Junius, for those unaware, was the pen name of an unknown British author of a series of masterful political letters published (1768-1772) in London, exposing the corruption of the British ministry and ineptitude of the King. It was the first effective blast directed at the heart of the royal power structure. It was an immediate sensation, for Junius not only reintroduced and popularized the classic polemic style of journalism, he was in effect, the 'Deep Throat' of the 1760s. He devastatingly revealed the court's dirty secrets and vowed to go to his grave without revealing the source of his information or his own true identity (much to the rage and frustration of his targets). The letters were collected by Woodfall the publisher in 1774 and issued in a two volume set, which was an immediate best seller, and is among the most popular political writings of the nineteenth century, as evidenced by the fact that almost every publisher at the time put out an edition. Rare is the rare bookstore of today that does not have a dusty, leather bound, two volume set of *Woodfall's Letters of Junius*. I consider each and every volume a work of Thomas Paine.

Again, without attempting to speak to the merits of Paine's authorship of these letters, I wish to point out the existence of such a case. There are some Paine detractors (Cheetham, Chalmers) that wish us to think that before coming to America he had no background of note and instead popped out of a (rum) bottle, immediately thereafter setting the political world on its head. Other modern detractors (Fast, Aldridge) portray Paine as popping up out of a London gutter. Biographers in general, with two notable exceptions (Denslow and Williamson), simply follow this unsavory lead and thus minimize the importance of Paine's life prior to his American phase, while imagining that immediately upon arriving in 1774 without significant writing experience, he secured the editorship of a leading literary journal, the *Pennsylvania Magazine*, wrote therein several absolutely original essays on human rights, and then wrote the all-time best selling self-help book on freedom – all without any meaningful literary background and, indeed, came to these shores precisely because he was a total failure at everything he had tried heretofore. Not likely so.

Biographers would like for us to believe that Paine's was a life of pure coincidence: As he was fortuitously residing in Philadelphia at the precise time that the Declaration was being written in the Spring of '76, so likewise he had just become situated in the environs of London at just the time that Junius commenced his journalistic attack; mysteriously the pen of Junius went silent at just the time that Paine moved out of London and relocated to Philadelphia. In fact, the pen of Junius did not skip a beat – he only changed his address, pen name, and broadened the scope of the issue. In addition to the books referring to Junius in the aforementioned list on the Declaration, there is one additional study which needs to be especially noted: William H. Graves, who (together with Denslow and Moody), makes the most complete case for Paine being the real Junius in *Junius Finally Discovered*, 1917.

In the nineteenth century, Denslow, in *Modern Thinkers*, provides a much needed review of Paine's background and connections prior to his coming to America. Of present day biographers, Audrey Williamson has presented the best study in this regard. Both reveal much new information concerning Paine's younger life that 'fits' the Junius profile. It is about time, in my opinion, for Paine biographers to acknowledge this old and new material, and open their eyes and recognize a fascinating and vitally important thesis pertaining to Paine scholarship. That this question also involves the truth concerning Junius, Jefferson, and our founding charter makes it a priority for research in the future. Nothing could be lost by this inquiry. Understanding would be gained and Thomas Paine could not as easily be ignored or disparaged. I am asking only that this inquiry be taken out of the rare book rooms and archives and put before the public for fair consideration.

As for the *artistic portraits* of Paine, the story of each individual canvas is as incongruous as the word portraits, if not more so. Thomas Paine's portrait was painted by almost all of the master portrait artists of his day in the three major countries, the U.S., England, and France. As of the end of WWII, there was not one single life portrait of Paine known to be in existence anywhere. What happened? This bizarre disappearance of irreplaceable artistic treasure would make an interesting sociological investigation in and of itself. I plan to pursue such a study in the future. Typically, Paine is the only founding father who lacks a definitive historical survey of his portraiture. I look forward with pleasure to correcting this glaring deficiency because in addition to discovery of new information is the possibility of finding more old portraits during my investigation.

Progress *is* being made with respect to locating original life portraits of Paine. Since WWII at least four major works have surfaced. John Trumbell painted a miniature portrait of Paine as a gift to Jefferson in 1788, together with a matching miniature portrait of Jefferson. Both miniatures hung together in the main parlor in Monticello during Jefferson's life. The Jefferson portrait hangs there now. The Paine miniature was lost when Jefferson's artifacts were dispersed in the 1840s. In the later 1940s, references to this painting were noted in the Jefferson Papers while they were being edited for the Library of Congress. The renewed interest led to its discovery in New England in a shoe box. It was the only life portrait then known to be in existence and was forthwith returned with great fanfare to Monticello, where it has remained safely out of sight in a desk drawer since 1948. It was brought out for a much needed restoration recently and a beautiful job was accomplished to ready it for public display. As mentioned, the Jefferson miniature has been hanging in the parlor all along, perhaps wondering what happened to its twin. It may also be wondering when its twin is going to be returned to its rightful place in the parlor. They are, after all, like two beautiful peas in a pod and should be hanging together as Trumbell obviously intended, and Jefferson effected. I have never been able to understand why these two masterpieces are not hanging together, where they belong. Therefore, I can be of no help in explaining this lack of historical and artistic sensitivity. I would suggest that your questions be directed to the Thomas Jefferson Memorial Society, which looks after Monticello and neglects the Paine miniature to this day.

The next painting to emerge was the portrait rendered by John Westley Jarvis in 1807 while Paine, at age 72, was residing in Jarvis's home in Greenwich Village. This painting was thought lost until one of Jarvis's biographies mentioned Paine's sitting for the portrait. A reader came forward in 1949 and said that the painting in question had been hanging in her home ever since she could remember. This painting was immediately donated with great fanfare by the family to the National Gallery of Art in Washington, D.C., where they stuck it in their storage basement and kept it there in the dark through the Bicentennial and up until 1983, whereupon, without being displayed once in the early American collection, it was summarily transferred over to the National Portrait Gallery, where all this time they had never acquired an oil portrait of Paine, though at least one to my knowledge was presented for their consideration.

In a way, the Smithsonian, which administers both galleries, managed to kill two birds with one bureaucratic stone: The National Gallery of Art staff was under pressure by the Thomas Paine Historical Society in Washington to display the Jarvis portrait and refused because they said it had no historical or artistic merit. Anyway, they got rid of it, and the National Portrait Gallery, to their credit, finally knew a good work of art when they saw one and promptly placed the work on permanent display, thus filling the artistic vacuum which had existed in their institution and in Washington, D.C. for many years. They think I should be happy with this arrangement but, at the risk of being greedy, the Jarvis portrait should, in my opinion, be returned to its rightful owner, the National Gallery of Art on the Mall and put on permanent display in the early American exhibit. They now have some forty Gilbert Stuart paintings hanging in this collection and not one Jarvis to be found. Since all major early American artists are supposed to be represented in this exhibit, such reinstatement and prominent exhibition would correct this oversight and bring Paine home to the Mall where he belongs. The National Portrait Gallery can then go out and find their own oil portrait of Paine, two of which (original life portraits) have been recently located by the writer. I will briefly mention each and close.

The first known life portrait of Thomas Jefferson was rendered by the British/American artist, Mather Brown, in London around 1785.

Jefferson liked the portrait so much that he commissioned Brown to paint his two good friends, John Adams and Thomas Paine. The Jefferson portrait by Brown (perhaps the best looking portrait of Jefferson) is now in the possession of the Adams family in New England. The famous John Adams portrait by Brown is now hanging in the Boston Atheneum Museum.

The Paine by Brown is in my possession as a result of its being offered in a family estate sale in Baltimore. More research needs to be done before this portrait can be conclusively shown to be Paine and attributed to Brown because its provenance is still a mystery. I am satisfied, based on appearance and comparison with known Paine life-portraits and with known Brown works, that it is the original Brown portrait of Paine commissioned by Jefferson.

The final life portrait to be mentioned is the most important. George Romney, in 1792, immortalized Paine by rendering the image with which we are now familiar in the history books and biographies. As soon as the painting was finished, it was engraved by William Sharp. It then disappeared and was thought to be lost forever. (In fact, Cooper, the original owner, brought it to America shortly after the commission.) The image survived, however, because Sharp's engraving was issued at the time of the publication of *Rights of Man*, which, it will be remembered, was one of the world's all-time best selling books. The unprecedented circulation of this particular image of Paine has led over the years to it being the stereotypical face that we all recognize. To my displeasure, it reflects a harsh, abrasive, almost smirking expression that was subtly engraved into the portrait by Sharp, apparently to enhance the sale by presenting a hard-nosed trouble-making façade of the author of *Rights of Man*. The original oil portrait by Romney was rediscovered by Moncure D. Conway, the foremost authority on Paine, at the turn of the century, and has ended up, blessedly, in the Thomas Paine Museum, headquarters of the Thomas Paine National Historical Association in New Rochelle, New York. It is especially pleasing to me that this original Romney portrait is now available to be seen by the public because, characteristic of the artist, it shows a very colorful, pleasant looking, philosophic Thomas Paine. Romney was not trying to sell engravings; he was painting his friend.

This portrait, believe it or not, has never been locked away since resurfacing, but has been on constant display by the Association since it was donated in 1927 and has been described by Van der Weyde as their most important possession. The attribution of this portrait to Romney has not yet been confirmed, but as Moncure Conway is my source, I am confident that its authenticity will stand up, hereafter changing for the better the public image of Paine. Biographers and historians, please take note.

As can be seen, the three-dimensional pursuit of Paine's portraits, as they emerge in newly discovered writings, canvasses, and interpretations, is an exciting and provocative quest. I could go on and relate additional horror stories of neglect and omission (such as the Paine portrait and bust being kicked out of Independence Square in Philadelphia by the National Park Service; or the adamant refusal to allow Paine's statue in Washington, D.C. or New York City), but I would rather end on the happy note of the George Romney and the Mather Brown portraits being rediscovered and now enjoyed in New Rochelle by those who care. I can only hope that from now on there is a greater willingness by academicians, bureaucrats, and citizens to respond to any new information regarding Paine as it is discovered or uncovered. It does no good to find lost portraits if they are not hung where people can see and appreciate them. Heretofore unattributed works such as the Junius letters and the Declaration of Independence must be proclaimed, first, to the open-minded and interested; and the closed-minded need to be challenged and corrected when they stand in the way of truth concerning our hero. We need Thomas Paine now, more than ever. We need all of the Paine we can get; artifacts, newly attributed writings, and fresh insights. I am glad that such a multi-dimensional portrait is still emerging.

I close by offering my own personal word portrait of Paine in form of contemporary lyrics of a song I have composed. The tune, as my friends involved with Paine know, is in my head.

THOMAS PAINE
Thomas Paine was the greatest name
In the Halls of History;
Yes, that's the way it was back then,
It's the way it ought now to be …
It's the way it ought now to be.

When he wrote *Common Sense*, its direct consequence
Was a great nation's liberty;

Thomas Paine

Now it's common silence,
A small nation's gratuity …
A small nation's gratuity.

'THESE ARE THE TIMES THAT TRY MEN'S SOULS.'
Immortal words he wrote when *Crisis* came;
And with this motto, going forth,
We overthrew the priest and the king …
We overthrew the priest and the king.

Jeff and George and John and (even) Ben
Were sore afraid to break away;
Until they were led by what Tom Paine said,
O were he here to lead us today …
O were he here to lead US today.

Now, tell me city bird, when last you laid your whitish turd
On the noble statued-head of Thomas P.?
God knows they're hard to find, but he's a friend of yours and mine
His *Rights of Man* and *Age of Reason* read …
His *Rights of Man* and *Age of Reason* read …

(Play it again, Dave)
Thomas Paine is the greatest name
In the Halls of History;
That's the way it is, my friend,
It's the way it ought to be …
It's the way it ought to be.

Robert Muller

Remarks on the Present State of the World, Inspired by the Philosophy of Thomas Paine

The series *Visionaries of World Peace* launched by UNIPAZ is a magnificent example of what that University can do. Not only does it revive the memory of great peacemakers throughout the ages, but it plays also the role of a University, of an educational institution. I knew little about Thomas Paine until this Colloquium was decided upon. Its preparation forced me to read a lot of his works and about him. The result was that I suddenly felt ashamed by the example of this extraordinary man who revealed to me that I had viewed my role as a peacemaker in a rather petty way. I thought that I was doing a lot for peace, having worked in the UN for forty years and always been at the forefront of building peace and new global instruments. I felt rather happy, content and proud of myself. And here enters into my life a man who shows me by his example that I was quite off the mark, that I should have been much more forceful, infinitely more audacious and less compromising with the prevailing beliefs, values, prejudices, and public opinion of my time. He emphatically stated that he would never allow public opinion to shape and influence his beliefs, that truth alone was his yardstick. He cut me up like a surgeon, reassembled me and made me a neo-revolutionary. That is why, in these few minutes, I will propose that you ask yourself this question as he would do if he were alive today:

Which are the seemingly impossible challenges of our age which Thomas Paine would raise to the sky with uninhibited courage and which will be solved in the decades or century ahead, as were those he raised in his time? This could be the practical outcome of this Colloquium. Let us put ourselves in the shoes of Thomas Paine, espouse his personality, and look at our present planetary and social conditions as he would do.

Since he was a technologist, he would certainly marvel at our scientific and technological achievements, at our planes, our satellites, our factories, our power plants, our universities, our computers, atomic bubble chambers, microscopes, telescopes, and so forth. He would be thrilled by the existence of the United Nations where all nations do meet for the first time. He would probably become a delegate to it! But, this being said, do you think that he would agree with the type of society and world disorder in which we live? Certainly not. He would slash through it exactly as he did at his time. He would look for the truth and denounce all prejudices and wrong beliefs, irrespective of dominant public opinion. He would give the world an agenda of major reforms for the next decade, century, and millennium which is only twelve years away. We must seek in our respective professions and walks of life what is basically wrong, what must be corrected on our evolutionary path, and what is the truth about our present human condition. I will highlight a few of these basic questions which are my 'Paine interrogations.' He dealt with the American and French Revolutions. Today he would deal with worldwide revolutions.

First, he would say: 'You know enormously about your planet, from outer-space to the inside of the atom, from the poles to the tropics, from the ozonosphere to the depths of the seas and oceans. You know all you need to know about humanity. You know for the first time how many people live on this planet, while we had no idea of it. You know how long people live in various parts of the world, their levels of health, nutrition, and education. What you know is prodigious, unprecedented in human evolution. You have for the first time in the human species' history good inventories of your planetary home and of the human race. But what do you do with this knowledge? Are you managing this planet well, now that you have become its masters? Are you creating the necessary harmony between the human species and the planet? I wrote in my time about the Rights of Man. Today I would write about the Rights of the Earth. I would draft a Declaration of the obligations of Man towards the planet. You are in a completely different situation. What you are doing is by and large endangering and damaging your planet. You call it "development," but when I look around I see more destruction than development.' He would write inflammatory pamphlets about that. He would open the eyes of the public to what we all perceive deep in our heart but do not dare to say, because of prevailing public opinion. He would show us the naked truth right away, while we are crawling painfully towards it through crisis after crisis. He would say that we have to manage this planet properly for the benefit of all, including future generations. Studying our political system, he would conclude that it is an obsolete mess, totally out of step with the interdependent needs of the planet and of humanity. He would ask, 'Why didn't you continue what was started in Philadelphia two hundred years ago? Why are you stuck? Why have you removed world political order from your preoccupations? You have no world law. You have no world parliament. You have no world equity. You have no world justice. You have no proper implementation of the global recommendations of your United Nations. You have totally wrong world priorities, spending a trillion dollars a year on planet-endangering arms while bickering about a few hundred million dollars for your indispensable, path-breaking world agencies. This is no way of managing a planet! If an inspection team came from outer-space, they would give you an F – failure – in planetary management. You have a UN, but you maintain, reinforce, and glorify a national 'sovereignty' system which renders the UN ineffective. Why don't you sit down and perfect, update, modernize the constitutional system we started in Philadelphia, extending it to the entire world, or at least to the Americas to start with? What did you do in Philadelphia during the Bicentennial of the US Constitution? You admired it, you glorified it, you had your mouths full of it. You had fireworks but you stopped at that, while the founding fathers would have looked at the entire world.'

My own recommendation, that the best thinkers should be brought together in Philadelphia to draft a constitution for the world, was not heard. A hundred young students, however, have constituted themselves as an association, *Philadelphia 2000*, to work on such a constitution. The gloomy prediction of Thomas Paine about the US and its lack of audacity is becoming true. Thanks God, we have the efforts of Ben Ferencz, a former prosecutor at the Nuremberg trials, who wrote a Common Sense manifesto which is being published in a million copies under the title *Planethood* by Ken Keyes, the author of the famous *One Hundredth Monkey*. Ben Ferencz is here with us. The Foreword of his book is being distributed to you.[109]

Thomas Paine would raise another fundamental question: the state of democracy in the world. He would say: 'How come that you have about sixty to seventy dictatorships – ideological dictatorships, military dictatorships, religious dictatorships? Why do you let democracy be corrupted through alliances between such dictatorships and special interest groups, for instance the merchants of death? Where is the people's will? Your people elect representatives with the special mandate to reduce or eliminate nuclear armaments and when they are in power they increase such arms! They promise to reduce budget deficits and at the end of their mandate, the deficit is bigger than before. You stick to national sovereignty in a global world where everything is interdependent, from the air to the waters, from nature to the human species. 'Sovereign' comes from king. You have a royal system of nations! We took the word sovereign away from the kings and gave it to the nation which was the right thing to do at the time. But today you must take it away from the nations and give it to the world and to humanity! You must declare national sovereignty an obsolete dictatorship and replace it by the peoples' sovereignty in a planetary home. You have to do at least for the world what the Europeans did when creating a European Community with supra-national powers. Since 1945 you went to the moon, you unlocked the atom, you performed incredible scientific achievements, but on the political front you produced only two timid advances: the United Nations and the European Community. You are giants in science and technology and pygmies in the political field. The two big powers seem to be sitting on the brains of all humans, preventing them from thinking. They occupy the world scene. I was busy dismantling the empires of the kings and we succeeded. You have new empires to dismantle and to establish a true world democracy of all peoples. Why don't you fight for a revolution in the relations and behavior of the two big powers, between the East and the West? Such groupings should realize that their divisions are harmful to the planet and cannot go on forever.'

If Thomas Paine went to Africa or Asia and saw the conditions in their poor countries, he would exclaim: 'It is unbelievable that such extreme conditions coexist on the same planet. In some parts of your world the people are suffocating in goods to the point that the human person disappears and the goods become all-important. And here people are lying in the streets, empty-handed and hopeless.' He would call not only for a revolution between East and West but also between North and South.

On human rights he would say: 'It is wonderful that you have written such beautiful and numerous additional texts since our 1789 *Declaration of the Rights of Man and of the Citizen* during the French Revolution. But how many have been ratified? How many clauses of escape have you tolerated? You have more violations of human rights on this planet than there are sins in hell. Why haven't you established a World Court of Human Rights to protect the individual against abuses by his government? Do you have a human right of governmental compliance with international treaties and the United Nations Charter? Have you thought of the human rights of future generations? Have you proclaimed the fundamental human right not to kill and not to be killed, not even in the name of a nation?'

Liberty having been one of his favorite subjects, he would ask: 'During your celebration of the Centennial of the Statue of Liberty, did you have the courage to raise the question of what liberty means today in your world? No, you refurbished the Statue, you had fireworks, but where was the philosophical discussion of the meaning of liberty in a world of powerful nations, of giant monopolies, of vast news media and advertisements which program the minds, needs, beliefs, and cultures of most of humanity?'

What is *freedom of information*, for example? I have to swallow *The New York Times* every day, but never has *The New York Times* published one of my letters of correction, disagreement, or protest. Where is *my* freedom, compared with the freedom of *The New York Times* when they publish slander against the United Nations? Just to give you an example: a few weeks ago they published an article on the 'gobbling of paper' by the UN 'paper mill.' A picture was shown of carriages loaded with paper entering the UN. I wrote to them asking them to inform their readers that the total UN documentation in *one year*, in five official languages, dealing with the most important subjects on Earth and never carrying one single advertisement, amounted to *one Sunday edition* of *The New York Times*! Do you think that they would ever publish such a letter? Margaret Mead, who never got her letters of defense of the UN published either, once suggested that a new newspaper should be launched which would publish the letters of readers rejected by *The New York Times.*

Reading Thomas Paine, I gained the conviction that he was a deeply spiritual person, a cosmic man who tried to find out what life was all about, what his personal cosmic responsibilities were as a human being. At the end of his life, he expressed his belief and contentment that 'he had tried to his best as a human being.' And this is what every human person should be able to say at the moment of death. He would probably say: 'You know so much at this stage of evolution, you should ask yourself a fundamental question, namely, what is life all about? What has God or the cosmos in mind for you on this planet? What do all your efforts and exertions mean? What is your future evolution going to be?

What is the destination of your journey on this miraculous planet in the vast fathomless universe? Why are humans born, why do you live, why do you die? Why does humanity accumulate all these experiences and knowledge? What is the future of this planet going to be?'

And he would probably address himself to the heads of states, especially those of the US and the USSR, and say: 'You have not only a responsibility towards your people and a responsibility towards the whole of humanity. You have also a responsibility towards God and the cosmos, because it depends upon you whether the cosmic experiment unfolding on this planet will continue or not.'

He would ask for a revolution in education, as Michael Foot did today. He would question us: 'What do you teach the children in your schools? Are they being taught that the world is their country, their home, and that humanity is their family? No, from all I can see your education starts with the nation and ends with it, as if it were an island floating alone on this planet. National glory, national history, national geography, national literature, national everything, plus the diminishing of other nations, especially competitors or potential enemies. How to do you expect to have responsible, non-violent citizens when you glorify and practice your own state violence and ignore the crying needs of the planet and of humanity? With ninety-nine percent of the youth of this planet being programmed in this way, how do you expect a peaceful and better world? You are suffering from illusions.'

He would be thrilled by the news that there is a first supra-national University for Peace located in a country that has constitutionally disarmed itself: Costa Rica. But he would be appalled to learn that the University is left penniless by nations who in the meanwhile pour huge resources in hundreds of military academies. He would think that we are mad.

He would advocate a revolution in the art of living, or the *art of being*, as he called it, revealing how deep his thinking went. He would ask: 'How come that the vast majority of your people are dissatisfied while your governments think that they are doing so well? Even in your rich countries the constant accumulation of goods and the creation of incessant dissatisfaction to produce more goods has led nowhere. Do you think that God or the cosmos has created humans to pile up goods? In your richest country, the United States, there are twenty million drug addicts! What other proof do you need of your failure to provide happiness and meaning to the people?'

Thomas Paine would point at the elements and exclaim: 'Who is representing and speaking for the atmosphere, for the waters, for the seas and oceans, for nature, for all other living species whom you destroy so recklessly?' He would be greener than the Greens and would surely start a world party of Greens to defend and save the Earth.

He would also ask: 'Why don't you have a world budget which would reveal to you what resources are devoted to what, and what colossal waste and distorted priorities there are in the use of the world's taxpayers' resources? Where are your plans for great dams, new canals, water and pipelines, and so forth, to improve the economic productivity of this planet, to regreen the deserts, to reforest the wastelands, to conserve your valuable resources? Again, what are these stupid, colossal military expenditures I see pop out of your budgets? Why don't you start a revolution against them?'

He would speak of the need for a revolution in the relations between the religions. He would ask why they still are the cause and allies of so many conflicts on this planet instead of offering their insights and wisdom to draft the cosmic or divine commandments for the behavior of individuals and institutions, above all nations, in order to uphold the sanctity and sacredness of human life.

I gave the above only as examples of some of the most important needed revolutions that came to my mind, but there are many others. They will occur to you, I am sure, in economics, in philosophy, in sociology, in biology, and so forth. There is scarcely a field of human endeavor which does not require a revolution due to the new global conditions and requirements of our planet.

In conclusion, may I point at a few dates which call for 'Painful' revolutionary rethinking of our human destiny, behavior, and political structure. There will be the Bicentennial of the French Revolution in 1989, the five hundredth anniversary of the discovery of the New World in 1992, and the Bimillennium celebrations in the year 2000. We must seize these occasions to draw conclusions and balance-sheets, to undertake deep, truthful, honest rethinking and revolutions for a better future and evolutionary duty. We go at present from anomaly to anomaly, from crisis to crisis, from accident to accident. This is no longer a proper way for a species that has reached our stage of evolution. I hope that you will leave this Colloquium with the firm determination to become a

Thomas Paine and to initiate deep-seated revolutions which might seem impossible today but which will all succeed as did those he undertook two hundred years ago against all odds and obstacles, for the good of humanity. May Thomas Paine relive in each of us.

Zofia Libiszowska

The Reality of the Constitutional Vision of Thomas Paine

Thomas Paine was not included into the galaxy of the Founding Fathers although that is where some of his biographers placed him.[110] Neither did he participate directly in the formulation of the 1787 Constitution or its propagation. At the time the Convention was starting in Philadelphia, he was already in Europe. He did neither take part in the Convention with famous politicians, nor with leaders of the patriot groups who were struggling for the independence of the United States, such as John Adams, Thomas Jefferson, and others known from the Congress debates.

The constitutional vision of 'the great absentee' exerted, however, a powerful impact on the debates of Congress. Great credit should be given here to Thomas Paine, who exhorted his fellow-citizens to abolish the British rule, while presenting his conception of the future Union. In Thomas Paine's vision presented in his pamphlet *Common Sense* (1776), America was to begin a new era in world history. Its government, compatible with the theory of natural law and rationalism, was to guarantee freedom and rights for individuals and for the whole nation. His famous statement was: 'The cause of America is in a great measure the cause of mankind.'[111]

The earlier conflict between Great Britain and its overseas colonies boiled down to the interpretation of the constitutional rights to which their inhabitants were entitled. They opposed the rights of British Parliament to issue official acts valid in America (Stamp Act, Declaratory Act). The incidents near Boston radicalized attitudes of both sides. Nobody questioned, however, the principles of the political system, shaped as a result of the 'Glorious Revolution,' which, at the time in Europe, was considered the model political system.[112]

Thomas Paine challenged that basic paradigm of his time and launched an attack on notions glorified by tradition. In introducing a distinction between society and government, Paine was abolishing a myth about the harmony, which supposedly was reigning between society and the British government since the time of the 'Glorious Revolution.' He submitted the British system to his total critical examination. According to him, the hereditary power of the king and lords was undermining the principles of the sovereignty of the people – leading to despotism, tyranny, and wars. Such a tyrant was George III. Monarchy and heredity were considered by Paine to be a constitutional error. Society had a right to overthrow its unworthy ruler and create its own government, he claimed. 'Our own government is our own natural Right.'[113] Sovereignty in this approach is an attribute of society and not of government.[114]

Thomas Paine demanded immediate proclamation of the Declaration of Independence, which, as an act legally adopted by Congress, would constitute a document of America's own national sovereignty and a guarantee of citizens' rights. Such a document would pave the way for establishing external relations allowing Americans to obtain economic independence from the metropolis. More than half a year was to pass before the decision about gaining independence was taken. *Common Sense* caused that it became inevitable, prepared minds for it, and exerted a direct influence on the content of the Declaration drafted by Thomas Jefferson.[115]

As a political thought theoretician, Thomas Paine was rejecting hereditary power, the principle of its three-tier division, and its aristocratic and monarchical elements. From the British system he accepted only its republican elements represented by the House of Commons. Under American conditions, its role was to be played by Congress – the representation of the sovereign nation.

Let us pass now to the constructive elements of his constitutional vision. It was to be the world's first realization of an Agreement by the people, to be drafted immediately after announcing independence. Not Great Britain but America would give the world a proper constitutional system. 'We have it in our power to begin the world over again … The birthday of a new world is at hand.'[116] Awareness of the crucial character of the events was deeply rooted in the public opinion. It is expressed in an inscription introduced to the Great Seal of the United States, *Novus Ordo Seclorum [new order of the ages/worlds]*.

The Constitution was to be a guarantee for preserving natural rights by society. It was to be a written document – the *Magna Carta Libertatum* – which was called *Continental Charter* by Paine. This document of highest rank was not to be drafted by the already debating Congress but by a special Constitutional Convention composed of delegates from each colony – members of the assemblies and delegates elected directly by all people – a combination of 'Knowledge and Power.'[117] The day on which the Constitution would be proclaimed was to be an especially solemn and festive day.

Years later he would return to the same subject, 'A constitution is not the act of its government, but of the people constituting a government, and government without a constitution is power without a right.'[118] Among fundamental natural rights, which should be guaranteed by the Constitution, he included the individual's right to liberty, property, and freedom of worship. The right to property was synonymous with the restrictions of the government's powers in the field of taxation.

The proposals concerning the structure of the future state were misty and utopian in 1776; but the main principles and ideas made their way into the consciousness of ordinary citizens. Among the most important of them was the idea of republicanism. Paine equipped the concepts of 'republic' and 'republicanism' with their new meanings. Historian Gordon S. Wood claims that until the year 1776 – and even later – these were terms with pejorative undertones. They were associated with memories of Cromwell's dictatorship. The writers in the Age of Enlightenment took an undecided stance towards republicanism. After all, the republics known from history had either collapsed, succumbed to rules of despots, or transformed themselves into governments of aristocratic oligarchies (Venice, Switzerland, Holland). Paine inspired the American society with faith in the republican system of government and unwillingness to monarchy. Implanting the spirit of republicanism or, in other words, The Spirit of Seventy Six into society along with the principle of sovereignty of people and the Union of the United Colonies, could be attributed, to a large extent, to Thomas Paine. The Spirit of Seventy Six was an appeal for national sovereignty, liberalism, and democracy.

Independence was to be decided upon through a referendum in each Colony, and each of them was to have the right to draft its own constitution. The Congress proposed this mode of deciding about the national future on the motion of John Adams. The most significant prerequisite of these decisions was to preserve the Union of Thirteen Colonies represented in Congress. The supreme authority of the Union was to remain with the one-house Congress. According to Thomas Paine's proposal, it was to be a congress-giant composed of representatives of all colonies in equal numbers. As a condition of egalitarianism, the author did not accept area or population size, but a geographical criterion. Provincial Assemblies were to subordinate themselves to decisions of the Congress.

The new State was to be a republic or, rather, a federation of republics. The king's place was to be taken by law, while law at each level was to be the people's will in Rousseau's sense. In Thomas Paine's conception, the term 'republicanism' was synonymous with the term 'democracy.' He voiced also in favor of eligibility for all adult men. That was a novel solution unknown in modern Europe. The elected President of the Union, or rather of Congress, was not to be the Chief of the executive authority. All power should belong to Congress. It is a conception of power of the people (democracy) leaving no room for separation of powers and all the more so to check and safeguard their balance. Executive power, according to Paine, 'can be considered in no other light than as inferior to the legislative. Sovereign authority in any country is the power to make laws, and everything else is an official department.'[119]

The constitutional vision of Thomas Paine in his further writings was enriched by new elements:

(a) Postulate about separation of the Church and the State
(b) Postulate about the abolition of slavery
(c) Postulate about the right for revision of the Constitution by future generations.

Each generation should have its right to amend the Constitution. The dead should not continue to govern from their graves. The same theses were advanced by Thomas Jefferson. Such a clause was introduced only into the Polish Constitution, adopted on May 3, 1791. It was one of the first constitutions in the late eighteenth century.

Thomas Paine was the first to formulate the name of the future State: *The United States of America*, and he supported firmly a close and inseparable Union. Moreover, he demanded a uniform federal citizenship. A state citizenship was considered by him to be an internal distinction.[120] He called himself a 'World Citizen.' The Republic was a 'Public Good,' he would explain.[121] Stable community and the Constitution guaranteeing the individual's rights would secure welfare for the country and create unlimited prospects for its development. Commerce and not politics or dynastic conflicts would ensure peace and security for the State and its concord with other countries.

In analyzing Thomas Paine's political theory it may be stated that it was a translation of the political philosophy of the Age of Enlightenment into an ordinary man's language. 'The power of Thomas Paine, though political, was not so much in what he said but in how he said it.'[122] Thomas Paine's constitutional vision crossed the Ocean and returned to his motherland. In Great Britain he is called the father of radicalism.[123] Indeed, in his polemic with Edmund Burke, Paine's views underwent a considerable radicalization. It was not Revolutionary France which he defended but instead he was proclaiming the universal revolution whose beginnings were the American Revolution and, in turn, the French Revolution. 'The Revolution in France is certainly a forerunner of the Revolution in Europe,' he wrote to Edmund Burke in January 1790.[124] He believed that the decaying British monarchy was drawing to its close and that the British people would become sovereign again. The French legislature included him among the honorable citizens of France. In 1792, as one of two foreigners (Kloots), he was elected to the National Convention and became a member of the Committee set up to draft the New Republican Constitution for France, which was headed by Danton. However, the members of the Committee made little use of the American model and ideas of Thomas Paine. He also opposed the bloody terror, being convinced – and he did not hesitate to voice the thesis – that abolition of the monarchy did not have to be combined with regicide.

In the opinion of the author of *Rights of Man*, the vision of sovereignty of the people and man's rights guaranteed by the Constitution were leading to brotherhood and universal peace. Thomas Paine believed that the War of Independence, although a just war, would be the last war fought by America. He also wanted to defend France from aggression by enemies of the Revolution; he was attempting to prove that republics were not inclined to aggression and war hostilities. He would give Poland as an example, which did not have a hereditary throne and fought far fewer wars than the hereditary monarchies.[125] According to him, a war was a whim of kings bringing misery and oppression of people. Such arguments can be found in the antiwar brochure *Prospects on the Rubicon* (1787) and in both volumes of *Rights of Man*.

Thomas Paine's ideas were taken over by the radical groupings of Great Britain in their publications. In the Bodleian Library, the collection of Undersecretary of State James Bland Burgess (Bland Burgess Papers), I found a leaflet printed in Leicester in September 1793, at the time that the war with France was already in progress.[126] The leaflet had been confiscated from a distributor of such leaflets, who was imprisoned immediately. The case was passed to the attorney-general, who ordered an investigation to find its author, who was using the pseudonym 'Hampden.' It is a leaflet printed on both sides, of newspaper size, and similarly to a newspaper it was printed in two columns. The title consisted of one word in capital spaced letters with three exclamation marks: 'W A R!!!' It resembles a call-word, an appeal, and summons. Its content was a passionate protest against the war which already had begun with the Republic of France. Arguments against the war included a threat of poverty, unemployment, decrease in production and trade. Here is a quotation: 'Will the murder of some thousands of Frenchmen be any consolation under these calamities?' ... 'Will the reestablishment of Absolute Monarchy in France ensure our future peace with that country? Will the dismemberment of France secure us from a visit of that infamous Combination whose treacherous conduct in Poland we are (to our eternal disgrace) indirectly giving a sanction to? Will the Christian Religion become more respected in France when propagated under the auspices of cannon and bayonets!'

Propaganda values of this fervent leaflet are a testimony of the author's writing skills. Its content and argumentation are convergent with the theses of the author of *Common Sense* and *Rights of Man*. A suspicion fell on Benjamin Vaughan who left Great Britain under penalty of imprisonment, while Thomas Paine was already in France. Whoever the author of this remarkable leaflet was, it stands to record that Thomas Paine's thought, lively and permanent, was reflected in its content. Under the heading 'WAR!!!' there is a motto: 'War is the pharo-table of Governments, and Nations are the dupes of the game,' and further on, 'War's a game that, were their subjects wise, kings would not play at' (*Rights of Man*, *Writings*, v. 1, p. 191). The famous sentence of Thomas Paine, 'These are the times that try men's souls' (*The American Crisis*, No. 1) was placed under the heading of the second article, 'The Effects of War on Poor.'

Along with the changing theatre of the European revolution, the republican constitutional vision of Thomas Paine was subject to reinterpretation. Thomas Paine's internationalist and antiwar slogans became the repertoire of radical circles in Great Britain, and they were persecuted by law. At that time, the French Revolution abandoned also the internationalist concept and appealed to national, patriotic feelings. The World Citizen and Defender of Man's Rights became a prisoner of Robespierre.

References

1 Russell Davenport, 'The California Spring,' in *American Caravan IV* (1931).
2 Leo Zonneveld, 'Teilhard de Chardin: A Search for the Unifying Power in Human Energy,' in *Humanity's Quest for Unity: A United Nations Teilhard Colloquium.* Leo Zonneveld, ed. First publication in the series of *Visionaries of World Peace*, in celebration of 40 years of the United Nations and the International Year of Peace, (The Hague: Mirananda Publishers, 1985).
3 Dag Hammarskjöld, *Markings*. Trans. W. H. Auden and L. Sjöberg, with a foreword by W. H. Auden (London: Faber and Faber Ltd., 1964), p. 31.
4 Plutarch, *De Exilio*, V.
5 Alan D. McKillop, 'Local Attachment and Cosmopolitanism – the Eighteenth-Century Pattern,' in *From Sensibility to Romanticism: Essays Presented to Frederick A. Pottle*, Frederick W. Hilles and Harold Bloom, eds. (New York: Oxford University Press, 1965), pp. 191-218.
6 For an excellent discussion of Stoic philosophy and world citizenship, see B. D. Shaw, 'The Divine Economy: Stoicism as Ideology,' *Latomus, vol. LXIV, no. 1* (1985), esp. pp. 28-30.
7 Paine's first extant letters were to Goldsmith and Franklin. See *The Complete Writings of Thomas Paine,* Philip S. Foner, ed. (New York: Citadel Press, 1945), vol. II, pp. 1129-32.
8 Quoted in Dumas Malone, *Jefferson and the Ordeal of Liberty* (Boston: Little, Brown and Co., 1962), p. 266.
9 *Boswell's Life of Johnson,* Frank Brady, ed. (New York: New American Library, 1968), p. 161.
10 *Common Sense* (1776), in *Complete Writings*, Foner, ed., vol. I, pp. 8-9, 19-20.
11 Ibid., pp. 3, 45.
12 Shortly after his return to England, Paine was made an honorary member of the Society for Constitutional Information.
13 See Albert Goodwin, *The Friends of Liberty: The English Democratic Movement in the Age of the French Revolution* (London: Hutchinson, 1979), pp. 110-12, 176-7, 245-67.
14 Quoted in Ibid., p. 250.
15 Ibid., pp. 110-11.
16 Joseph Priestley, *Letters to the Honourable Edmund Burke Occasioned by His Reflections on the Revolution in France* (Birmingham, 1791).
17 *Discourse on the Love of Our Country* (1789). Quoted in Goodwin, *Friends of Liberty*, p. 107.
18 *Reflections on the Revolution in France* (1790). Conor Cruise O'Brien, ed. (Harmondsworth: Penguin, 1969), p. 91.

19 On circulation figures see E. P. Thompson, *The Making of the English Working Class* (Harmondsworth: Penguin, 1963), pp. 102, 118-25.
20 For Paine's appeal for a 'confederation of nations and an European Congress,' see *Rights of Man* (1791-2), Henry Collins, ed. (Harmondsworth: Penguin, 1969), p. 67.
21 Thompson, *Making of the English Working Class*, pp. 122-4; Ian Dyck, 'Debts and Liabilities: William Cobbett and Thomas Paine,' in *Citizen of the World: Essays on Thomas Paine* (London: Christopher Helm, 1987), p. 96; H. T.; Dickinson, *British Radicalism and the French Revolution* (Oxford: Basil Blackwell, 1985), p. 35.
22 Eric Foner, *Tom Paine and Revolutionary America* (New York: Oxford University Press, 1976), pp. 239-41.
23 Paine to James Monroe, 10 September 1794, in *Writings*, Foner, ed., vol. II, pp. 1345-54.
24 See, for example, *Writings*, Foner, ed., vol. II, p. 1348 n. 244.
25 [William Cobbett], *Porcupine's Works* (London, 1801), Vol. IV, pp. 112-13.
26 'To the People of England on the Invasion of England' (1804), in *Writings*, Foner, ed., vol II, pp. 675-83.
27 'The Sons of Albion' (Cambridge University Library, Madden Collection of Ballads, XVII). For the cultural dimension of the anti-Gallican reactions of the 1790s and early 1800s, see Gerald Newman, *The Rise of English Nationalism* (New York: St. Martin's Press, 1987), pp. 231-3.
28 See *The Age of Reason* in *Writings*, Foner, ed., vol. I, pp. 463-604.
29 Jerome D. Wilson and William F. Ricketson, *Thomas Paine* (Boston: Twayne Publishers, G. K. Hall & Co., 1978), p. 128.
30 Vernon Parrington, *Main Currents in American Thought,* volume I, The Colonial Mind (New York: Harcourt, Brace & Jovanovich, 1930), p. 341.
31 Alfred Owen Aldridge, *Man of Reason: The Life of Thomas Paine* (Philadelphia: J. B. Lippincott Co., 1959), p. 34.
32 Ibid, p. 53.
33 *Encyclopedia Britannica*, 15th Edition, Vol. 13.
34 Aldridge, *Man of Reason*, p. 191.
35 Ibid.
36 Ibid.
37 E*ssential Writings of Thomas Paine*, Sidney Hook, ed. (New York: New American Library, 1969).
38 Philip S. Foner, ed., *The Complete Writings of Thomas Paine*, Two Vols., 1945 (New York: Citadel Press, 1969).
39 Parrington, *Main Currents in American Thought*, p. 341.
40 Foner, *The Complete Writings of Thomas Pain*e, p. 328.
41 Ibid.

42 Aldridge, *Man of Reason*, p. 322.
43 Wilson and Ricketson, *Thomas Paine*, p. 133.
44 Among useful works which isolate one aspect of Paine's thought are: Joseph Dorfman, 'The Economic Philosophy of Thomas Paine,' *Political Science Quarterly*, LIII (September, 1938), pp. 372-86; Howard Penniman, 'Thomas Paine – Democrat,' *American Political Science Review*, XXXVII (April, 1943), pp. 244-62; Harry Hayden Clark, 'Toward a Reinterpretation of Thomas Paine,' *American Literature*, V (May, 1933), pp. 133-45. David Freeman Hawke, *Paine* (New York: Harper and Row, 1974) is now the best one-volume biography, but Moncure D. Conway, *The Life of Thomas Paine*, 2 Vols. (New York: G. P. Putnam's Sons, 1892) is still useful. See also Eric Foner, *Tom Paine and Revolutionary America* (New York: Oxford University Press, 1976), which develops at greater length themes of this paper.
45 *Memoirs de Madame Roland* (2 vols.: Paris, 1834 ed.), II, p.295.
46 Philip S. Foner, ed., *The Complete Writings of Thomas Paine*, 2 vols. (New York: The Citadel Press, 1945), I, pp. 4-16, 29, II, p. 1480; W. Paul Adams, 'Republicanism in Political Rhetoric Before 1776,' *Political Science Quarterly*, LXXXV (September, 1970), pp. 398-404.
47 Foner, *Complete Writings*, I, pp. 16-21, 25-26, 31-32, 41, 44-45.
48 Thomas R. Adams, *American Independence: The Growth of an Idea* (Providence: Brown University Press, 1965), pp. xi-xii; L. H. Butterfield, ed., *Diary and Autobiography of John Adams,* 4 vols. (Cambridge: Belknap Press of Harvard University Press, 1961), III, p. 333; Charles Inglis, *The True Interest of America* (Philadelphia: Printed and sold by James Humphreys Jr., 1776), p. 34; Bernard Bailyn, *Ideological Origins of the American Revolution* (Cambridge: Belknap Press of Harvard University Press, 1967), pp. 12-19.
49 Elisha P. Douglass, *Rebels and Democrats* (Chapel Hill: University of North Carolina Press, 1955), p. 21; Foner, *Complete Writings*, I, p. 260, II, p. 78, 111.
50 Foner, *Complete Writings*, I, p. xviii. See also the excellent discussions of Paine's literary style in E. P. Thompson, *The Making of the English Working Class* (London: V. Gollancz, 1963), pp. 90-92; Harry Hayden Clark, 'Thomas Paine's Theories or Rhetoric,' *Transactions*, Wisconsin Academy of Sciences, Arts and Letters, XXVIII (1933), pp. 307-09; James T. Boulton, *The Language of Politics in the Age of Wilkes and Burke* (London: Routledge and K. Paul, 1963).
51 Hawke, *Paine*, p. 47; Gwyn Williams, *Artisans and Sans-Culottes* (New York: Norton, 1969); *To the Free and Patriotic Inhabitants of the City of Philadelphia*, Broadside, May 31, 1770; 'A Lover of Liberty and a Mechanic's Friend,' *Pa. Gazette*, September 27, 1770; Charles H. Lincoln, The *Revolutionary Movement in Pennsylvania 1760-1776* (Philadelphia: The

University, 1901), p. 80n.; R. A. Ryerson, 'Political Mobilization and the American Revolution: The Revolutionary Movement in Philadelphia, 1765 to 1776,' *William and Mary Quarterly*, 3 ser., XXXI (October, 1974), pp. 565-88.
52 The best account of Paine's early life is in Audrey Williamson, *Thomas Paine, His Life, Work and Times* (New York: George Allen and Unwin Ltd., 1974), pp. 11-59.
53 Hawke, *Paine*, p. 71; Foner, *Complete Writings*, I, p. 32, II, pp. 90, 202, 241-2, 1292.
54 See Charles S. Olton, 'Philadelphia Artisans and the American Revolution' (unpublished doctoral dissertation, University of California, Berkeley, 1967).
55 Foner, *Complete Writings*, I, p. 412.
56 Ibid., I, pp. 9, 203, 326, 343, 618-20.
57 Ibid., I, p. 397; Arthur O. Lovejoy, *Reflections on Human Nature* (Baltimore: Johns Hopkins Press, 1961), pp. 50-65; W. Stark, *America: Ideal and Reality* (London: K. Paul, 1947), pp. 100-05.
58 Foner, *Complete Writings,* I, pp. 404-05, 424-31; Caroline Robbins, 'European Republicanism in the Century and a Half Before 1776,' in *The Development of a Revolutionary Mentality,* Symposium 1972 (Washington: Library of Congress, 1972), p. 50.
59 J. R. Pole, *Political Representation in England and the Origins of the American Republic* (New York: St. Martin's Press, 1966), pp. 475-77; Place Collection, British Museum Add. MSS 27, p. 814 f. 29; *Proceedings of the Public Meeting Held in Sheffield* ... (Sheffield, 1974), pp. 29-30; Carl B. Cone, *The English Jacobins* (New York: Scribner, 1967), p. 227; LCS Address, August 6, 1792, PRO: TS 11/958/3503.
60 Thompson, *Making*, p. 90.
61 Hawke, *Paine*, p. 7.
62 'Letter to Henry Laurens' (Spring 1778), in Philip S. Foner, ed., *The Complete Writings of Thomas Paine*, 2 vols. (New York: The Citadel Press, 1945), II, p. 1143.
63 Ibid., p.303.
64 Alfred Owen Aldridge, *Man of Reason: The Life of Thomas Paine* (Philadelphia & New York: Lippincott, 1959), p. 99.
65 'Reflections on Titles,' Foner, II, p. 33.
66 'Thoughts on Defensive War,' Foner, II, p. 53.
67 Ibid.
68 *Common Sense*, Foner, I, p. 17.
69 *American Crisis* III, Foner, I, p. 94.
70 Ibid., p. 93.
71 *Maritime Compact*, Foner, II, p. 946.

72 Ibid., p. 941.
73 Ibid., p. 944.
74 Ibid., p. 945.
75 Ibid., p. 946.
76 *Letter to the Abbé Raynal*, Foner, II, p. 262.
77 See D. Abel, 'The Significance of the *Letter to the Abbé Raynal* in the Progress of Thomas Paine's Thought,' *Pennsylvania Magazine of History and Biography*, LXVI (April 1942), pp. 176-190.
78 *Letter to the Abbé Raynal*, Foner, II, p. 241.
79 Ibid., p. 256.
80 Ibid., p. 244.
81 Ibid.
82 Ibid., p. 245.
83 Ibid., p. 242.
84 Ibid., p. 244.
85 Thomas Paine, *Rights of Man* (Harmondsworth: Penguin Books, 1969), p. 289.
86 Ibid., p. 288.
87 'To the People of England on the Invasion of England,' Foner, II, p. 680.
88 Historical Manuscript Commission, *The Manuscript of J. B. Fortescue preserved at Dropmore*, 10 vols. (London, 1894), IV, p. 70.
89 'Letter addressed to the Addressers on the Late Proclamation,' Foner, II, p. 488.
90 *Letter to the Abbé Raynal*, Foner, II, p. 238.
91 Woodrow Wilson, *A History of the American People*, Vol. III (New York; Harper and Brothers, 1917), p. 91.
92 John C. Miller, *Origins of the American Revolution (*Boston: Little, Brown and Co.), p. 467.
93 Maurice Rovner, *Master Units of American History*, p. 27.
94 James T. Adams, *Revolutionary New England, 1691-1776* (Boston: Little, Brown, in association with Atlantic Monthly), p. 439.
95 Richard Frothingham, *The Rise of the Republic of the United States* (Boston: Little, Brown and Co, 1881), p. 479.
96 Catherine Bowen, *John Adams and the American Revolution* (Boston: Little Brown, 1954), p. 560.
97 W. E. Woodward, *A New American History* (New York: Farrar and Rinehart, Inc., 1936), p. 158.
98 Charles A. Beard and Mary R. Beard, *The Rise of American Civilization* (New York: Macmillan, 1945), p. 261.
99 Victor Robinson, *Lives of Great Altrurians, William Godwin and Mary Wollstonecraft* (New York: The Altrurians, 1908), p. 4.

100 Elbert Hubbard, *Little Journeys to the Homes of Great Reformers*, Vol. XX, (East Aurora, NY: The Roycrofters, 1907), p. 138.
101 Philip S. Foner, *The Life and Major Writings of Thomas Paine* (Bridgewater, NJ: Replica Books, Baker & Taylor, 1999), p. xiii.
102 W. E. Woodward, *Tom Paine: America's Godfather 1737-1809* (New York: E. P. Dutton and Co., 1945), p. 79.
103 Robert G. Ingersoll, *An Oration on the Life and Service of Thomas Paine* (Fairbury, Il, January 30, 1871), p. 124.
104 Oscar S. Straus, *Thomas Paine, Foremost Constructive Statesman of His Time*, (New York: Thomas Paine National Historical Association, 1921), p. 15.
105 John E. Remsburg, *Six Historic Americans: Paine, Jefferson, Washington, Franklin, Lincoln, Grant, and Fathers and Saviors of our Republic* (New York: The Truth Seeker Co., 1906), p. 16.
106 Thomas A. Edison, quoted from introduction of Wm. M. Van der Weyde's *The Life and Works of Thomas Paine*, Vol. I.
107 Thomas Jefferson, November 29, 1775 in a letter to John Randolph, *Papers of Thomas Jefferson*, Vol. I, p. 152.
108 Thomas Paine, *Common Sense*, January 9, 1776.
109 Benjamin B. Ferencz with Ken Keyes, Jr., *Planethood*, (Coos Bay, Oregon: Vision Books, 1988).
110 Francis Kercheville Hail, *Thomas Paine: Interpretative Study on the Treatment of Paine by Biographers, Historians and Critics* (Ann Arbor University, 1971).
111 Philip S. Foner, ed. *The Complete Writings of Thomas Paine* (New York: The Citadel Press, 1945), further quoted as *Writings*. v. 1, p. 2.
112 Gordon S. Wood, *The Creation of the American Republic, 1776-1787* (Chapel Hill, N.C. University of North Carolina Press, 1969), pp. 10 and 44.
113 *Writings*, p. 29. See also Bernard Bailyn, 'Common Sense' in *Fundamental Testaments of the American Revolution*, Papers presented at the Second Symposium (Library of Congress, Washington, D.C., 1974), pp.14-17.
114 G. S. Woods, op cit., p. 225. Also J. P. Diggins, *The Lost Soul of American Politics, Virtue, Self-interest and Foundations of Liberalism* (New York: Harper Collins, 1984), p. 38.
115 Albert Matthews, 'Thomas Paine and the Declaration of Independence.' *Massachusetts Historical Society*, v. 43, 1910, p. 241. Also Joseph Lewis, *Thomas Paine, Author of the Declaration of Independence* (New York: Freethought Press Association, 1947), p. 306.
116 *Writings*, op.cit., v. 1, p. 45.
117 *Writings*, op.cit., v. 1, p. 28. See also Owen Aldridge, *Thomas Paine's American Ideology* (Newark: University of Delaware Press, 1984), the best monography on Thomas Paine's political thought.

118 *Rights of Man, Writings,* op.cit., p. 375
119 *Rights of Man* (Everyman Ed.) p. 207. See also Charles. C. Thach, *The Creation of the Presidency, 1775-1789* (Baltimore: Da Capo Press, 1969), p. 30.
120 See *Letters to Rhode Island,* nr 1 and 3, *Writings,* v. 2, pp. 345-366; Also *The American Crisis XIII*, 19 IV 1783, *Writings,* v. 1, pp. 230-235.
121 'Public Good,' Philadelphia, 30 XII, 1781, *Writings,* v. 2, pp. 303-332.
122 See A. Ladousse, 'La rétorique comme ideologie dans Common Sense.' *Annales du Centre de Recherches sur l'Amérique* (Bordeaux, v. III, nr 3, 1974). See also F. K. Hail, op.cit., p. 314.
123 See Z. Libiszowska, 'Radykalizacja pogladów Tomasza Paine' [The Growth of Radicalism in the Political Thought of Thomas Paine], *Acta Universitatis Lodziensis,* ser. 1 nr 28, 1978. Also by the same author: *Tomasz Paine Obrońca Praw Czlowieka* [Thomas Paine, Defender of Human Rights], (Warszawa, 1976).
124 T. Paine to E. Burke, Paris 17 I 1790, *Burke, The Correspondence*, v. VI, ed. A. Coggan and R. A. Smith (Cambridge: Cambridge University Press, 1967), p. 71.
125 'Poland, through elective monarchy, has had fewer wars than those which are hereditary; it is the only government that made a voluntary effort, albeit but a small one, to improve the condition of the country.' See Harry H. Clark, ed., *Thomas Paine* (New York, Hill and Wang, 1961), p. 188.
126 Bodleian Library, Oxford, *J. Bland Burgess Papers*. Special Correspondence N-T (dissoluta). It was published as an appendix to my paper 'The Growth of Radicalism,' op.cit.

Photographs taken at the Colloquium

Left to right: Rodrigo Carazo, Leo Zonneveld, Ian Dyck, Bonnie Corso and Sean Wilentz. Between Bonnie Corso and Sean Wilentz: Mrs Robert Muller and Mrs Elinore Detiger.

Left to right: Leo Zonneveld, Michael Foot, Sean Wilentz, Ian Dyck, Charles Francisco, Bernard Vincent, David Braff, Clive Phillpott, Florence Stapleton, David Henley, Paul O'Dwyer and Robert Muller.

Thomas Paine

Florence Stapleton

Clive Phillpot

Leo Zonneveld

Contributors

MICHAEL FOOT (England), b. 1913. English politician and writer, leader of the Labour Party 1980-1983. President of the Thomas Paine Society, UK.

IAN DYCK (Canada), 1954-2007. Professor of History in Saskatoon and Lethbridge and from 1988 at Simon Fraser University. Writer and editor of books, including *Citizen of the World: Essays on Thomas Paine* (1988) and *William Cobbett and Rural Popular Culture* (2005), as well as collections, articles, and reviews. Outstanding teacher.

DAVID BRAFF (United States), b. 1947. Background and involvement in history and world affairs.

ERIC FONER (United States), b. 1943. Historian, Professor of American History at Columbia University, former president of the Organization of American Historians and president of the American Historical Association. Among his many books are *Tom Paine and Revolutionary America* (1976) and *Paine: Collected Writings* (1995). His father was historian Jack D. Foner and his uncle was Philip S. Foner to whose *Life and Major Writings of Thomas Paine* and *Complete Writings of Thomas Paine* (1945) several of the presenters refer.

CHARLES FRANCISCO (United States). Popular television actor in the 1960s. Author of several books, including *David Niven: Endearing Rascal* (1986).

BERNARD VINCENT (France). Professor Emeritus at the University of Orléans. Author of *The Transatlantic Republican, Thomas Paine and the Age of Revolutions* (2005).

CLIVE PHILLPOT (England, United States). Born in England, came to the US and became director of the Museum of Modern Art library in New York City, then returned to England as a freelance writer and art library and archive consultant. Author of essays about artists and their work.

PAUL O'DWYER (Ireland, United States), 1907-1998. Progressive lawyer and activist, involved in New York City politics and in workers' rights and civil rights in the US and elsewhere, including republicanism in Ireland. He served as president of the New York City Council (1974-1978) and, as he mentions, received the Thomas Paine Award from the National Emergency Civil Liberties Committee.

SEAN WILENTZ (United States), b. 1951. Historian and Professor of History at Princeton University. His scholarship has focused on the early years of the American republic, including a major study, *The Rise of American Democracy: Jefferson to Lincoln* (2006). Also a social/political commentator on current issues, contributing to *The New Republic* and *Rolling Stone*.

DAVID HENLEY (United States). Thomas Paine historian. Major participant in the Thomas Paine National Historical Association and to Thomas Paine Friends, making presentations and contributing articles on current Thomas Paine research and commemorations, as well as on other free thinkers in the spirit of Thomas Paine.

ROBERT MULLER (Belgium/France, United States, Costa Rica), b. 1923. Served forty years at the United Nations, rising to Assistant Secretary-General. Called the 'Prophet of Hope' of the UN and the 'father of global education,' having developed a 'World Core Curriculum' that is taught in Robert Muller schools around the world. In an active retirement, he has served as Chancellor of the University for Peace created by the UN in demilitarized Costa Rica. He has written many books, including *Most of All They Taught Me Happiness* (1978 and 2005). With his wife Barbara, Muller has a daily (M-F) 'GoodMorning' email message for creating a better world. His website is www.robertmuller.org.

ZOFIA LIBISZOWSKA (Poland). Historian and writer, whose works include *Tomasz Jefferson* (1984) and various contributions to the understanding and influence of Thomas Paine.

JOYCE CHUMBLEY (United States). Employment Specialist for Older Workers, Independent Researcher and Writer, Climate and Environmental Campaigner, Arts Council Director, Educational Consultant, College Instructor, and Dean … idea composter … co-learner … wholistic networker … impresaria of celebrations … globalist.

Correspondence

Correspondence between Florence Stapleton and Leo Zonneveld in Planning the Thomas Paine Colloquium

Following a visit on Saturday, April 4, 1987, made by Leo Zonneveld and two friends, Bonnie Corso and Lisa Sperling, to New Rochelle, New York, where they were given a tour of the Thomas Paine Cottage by Florence Stapleton, Leo and Florence began a correspondence. Excerpts follow.

Florence to Leo – May 3, 1987
The paper you sent me drawing the bond between Teilhard de Chardin and Paine brings out a deeper value of the Patriot's mind than I realized.

Leo to Florence – May 26, 1987
There is the human mind, co-partner, co-operator, co-creator with the universal mind.

Florence to Leo – August 20, 1987
The opportunity you presented the Association [Thomas Paine National Historical Association] *through me yesterday and confirmed this morning of placing Thomas Paine before the world via the United Nations – is overwhelming!*

But this is too great an opportunity to honor such a great friend of mankind to miss. I shall inform the President of our Association and advise Marina Kaufman [Friends of the University for Peace Foundation, New York] *and Mr. Ostrowski* [Krzysztof Ostrowski, Executive Secretary of the United Nations 1986 International Year of Peace and Peace Research Section] *of your proposal, viz: to call together six or seven 'Painites' to give addresses (30 minutes) at the U.N. on a date to be selected late November (after 11-17) through December, 1987 – the 250th anniversary year of Thomas Paine!*

Knowing, as you do, that, though a recent President, I am not on the Executive Committee; that we are an all-volunteer group without great financial resource, but which has extraordinary heritage spiritual as well as actual documents from the founders of 1906. You are courageous to call me!

Little people are sometimes called to do great things. Thanks for the opportunity to try.

Leo to Florence – August 28, 1987
[There is] *a possible opening to hold a Colloquium on Thomas Paine – provided we can do it before the end of the year!*

Attached I am sending you some briefing material on the Teilhard Conference in 1983, from which you can see the format and scope of this first Conference. With a bit of luck and support from the Almighty, Paine may become the second visionary in the series ...

If you think you can get 7-10 people together to speak on Paine and his work for peace for a date in October/November in the United Nations Headquarters then I will inform the whole network that the Colloquium is on. It will be held under the auspices of the UN University for Peace and my small organization called the United Teilhard Trust and supported by the UN Peace Studies Unit, led by Mr. Ostrowski.

I will care for the infrastructure of the whole event, if you like.

P.S. Bonnie will help you! [Bonnie Corso, then representing the United Teilhard Trust]

Florence sent an outline of the program to Marina Kaufman and to Krzysztof Ostrowski, but they did not reply. Florence became temporarily discouraged.

Florence to Leo – August 31, 1987
I have had no response ... and consider the prospect closed.

This is rather a heartache, but well worth the thought. With time and expertise it could be an extraordinary event. Friends of Thomas Paine, past and present, are very generous with their time and talent to honor a man who has been so enormously ignored.

Leo interceded and the prospect for a Thomas Paine Colloquium was not closed. It gained a distinct focus.

Florence to Leo – September 1, 1987
Your letter of August 28 arrived today ... It brings the background I needed to understand your 'vision.' Peace must be the central theme. Although peace is the ultimate goal for his Religion de la Liberté, for his

daring battles of words and actions to tear down the enemies in church and state that have enslaved mankind – it would take devoted research and development throughout his writings to establish the theme. As you see by the suggested titles on my list of speakers, controversy is the element dominant. The great humanist is seen as a rebel (ironic!) – for the causes of equality and peace among men. Even I have never thought of his contributing to peace as a central expression. I don't think of numerous passages in his writings such as near the end of Common Sense: 'Let the names of Whig and Tory be extinct and none other be heard – than good citizen – resolute friend – virtuous supporter of the rights of mankind.' Through many of his pages – ! The Maritime Contract [Maritime Compact,1800] *stands out ... Could we but have time to write and invite these speakers and many not listed if they could consider this subject: Paine, Apostle of Universal Peace.*

The list of speakers was confirmed; the venue was secured; and the Thomas Paine Colloquium was on!

Florence to Leo – July 14, 1988 (after the event)

Le 14 juillet 1988: Could this be the beautiful day, the hour longed for? For one July 4 and 14 symbolize events of giant proportions precipitated by the pen of one man. Time had found him and the elements were there! When will time find me? Am I destined to fulfill my longing to tell you and Bonnie what your visit at the Museum did for me one spring day in 1987!

Name and Subject Index

A Friend to Rhode Island and the Union 55
Adams, John 39, 44, 47, 51, 54, 106, 108, 117, 119
Adams, Samuel 60
Addison, Joseph 32
Age of Enlightenment 11, 15, 119, 120
Age of Revolution 44, 89
Agrarian Justice 30, 61, 63
Aldridge, Alfred Owen 71, 103
Alford, England 72, 77, 78
American Crisis 32, 40 57-58, 97-98, 108, 122
American Philosophical Society Library 102
American Revolution 13, 25, 33-34, 39, 44, 53-54, 70, 92, 97, 99, 110, 121
animal rights 97
Arias Sánchez, Óscar 17, 18
Asgill, Captain 40
Association of Nations 14, 16, 17, 32, 62, 66, 97
Attenborough, Richard 26
Ayer, Alfred 26
Bank of (North) America 49-50, 97
Barlow, Joel 91-92
Battle of Lexington 65
Beard, Charles 71
Bimillennium 115
Birmingham Six 86
Blake, William 70
Bolingbroke, Viscount 32
Born Yesterday 96
Boston Atheneum Museum 106
Braff, David 9, 13, 39, 132
Brissot, Jacques Pierre 36
bridges 73, 93, 97
British Jacobins 35-36
Brown, Mather 105-207
Bunyon, John 91, 93
Burges, James Bland 121
Burke, Edmund 35, 48, 58, 121
Carazo Odio, Rodrigo 9, 18, 22
Chalmers, George 102

Chartists 91
Cheetham, James 91-92
Chumbley, Joyce 1, 7, 133
Citizen of the World 12, 16, 29, 32, 34-36, 38, 42, 75, 120, 122
citizenship 37, 71, 120
Cobbett, William 26, 27, 37, 71
Commager, Henry Steele 71, 87, 88
Common Sense 11, 13, 15, 17, 33, 39, 45, 46-47, 49, 50, 56-57, 72, 94, 97-100, 101, 117-118, 122
Constitutional Society, Birmingham 34
Continental Convention 15, 64, 99, 118
Conway, Moncure D. 26, 106-107
Condorcet, Marquis (Jean Andre De Luc) 36
Costa Rica 7, 17, 21, 114
Cromwell, Oliver 46
Danton, Georges-Jacques 121
Davenport, Russell 20
De Tocqueville, Alexis 91
Declaration of Independence 15, 28, 34, 39, 61, 64, 84, 97-98, 100-102, 107, 118
Declaration of the Rights of Man and of Citizens 90, 97, 112
Deism 27, 37, 41, 53, 97
democracy 11, 12, 16, 18, 24, 25, 36, 49, 90, 92, 94, 95, 111, 112, 119, 120
Denslow, Van Buren 102-103
Dewey, John 16
Diderot, Denis 74
Doherty, Joe 88
Dyck, Ian 9, 12, 32, 132
Ernst, Maurice 21
Fast, Howard 85, 103
Ferencz, Benjamin 111
Ferguson, Marilyn 21
Fisher, Linda 87
Foner, Eric 9, 13, 44, 71-72, 132
Foner, Philip S. 26
Foot, Michael 9, 12, 23, 91, 114, 132
Founding Fathers 22, 39, 74, 117
Francisco, Charles 13, 55, 132
Franklin, Benjamin 33, 44, 89, 108
Frazee, John 92
French Revolution 13, 14, 34, 37, 40, 45, 49, 58, 70, 90-91, 97, 110, 112

Gandhi, Mohandas 65
George III 118
George, Henry 94
Girodins 14, 36, 41, 91
Goldsmith, Oliver 32-33
Gorbachev, Mikhail 12, 23-24, 29-30
Graves, William H. 103
Greenwich Village 87, 105
Guizot, Francois 91
Habermas, Jürgen 16
Hamilton, Alexander 44
Hammarskjöld, Dag 21
Hawke, David Freeman 49
Henley, David 10, 15, 96, 133
Hogarth, William 74
House Committee on UnAmerican Activities 85
Houston, Jean 21
Huddy, Captain 40
Hume, David 11
independence 39-40, 46, 56, 64, 97, 99
Ingersoll, Robert G. 128
International Association of Democratic Lawyers 86
International Year of Peace 19
internationalism 37, 44, 66, 97
Irish Rebellion 83
Jackson, Andrew 92
Jacobins 36, 37, 90, 91
James II 35
Jarvis, John Wesley 73, 105
Jefferson, Thomas 14, 17, 27, 28, 33-34, 37, 44, 49, 62, 92, 101, 104-106, 108, 117-118, 120
Johnson, Samuel 33
Kant, Immanuel 11
Keitel, Harvey 72
Keyes, Jr., Ken 111
La Nuit de Varennes 72
Landsdowne, Marquis of 68
Latour, Bruno 16
Laurens, Henry 47
Letter to Mrs. Few of Bordentown, NJ 63
Letter to Samuel Adams 60

Letter to the Abbé Raynal 66, 67
Lewes, England 49, 79, 80, 81, 82, 89
Lewis, Joseph 102
Libiszowska, Zofia 10, 15, 117, 133
Lincoln, Abraham 92
Livingston, Robert R. 87-88
Locke, John 35
London Corresponding Society 34, 52
Louis XVI 37, 41, 59-60, 72, 85, 90
Louisiana Territory 97
Ludwig, Robin 9, 19
Luxembourg Prison 91
Madison, James 51
Magna Carta 86
Marat, Jean-Paul 41
Marie Antoinette 40
Maritime Compact 62, 66
Marx, Karl 91
Mather, Joseph 89
Mencken, H. L. 94
military invasion of England 65
Mills, Nat 7-8
Milton, John 16, 91
Moleville, A. F. Bertrand de 40
Monroe, James 12, 87
Moody, Joel 101, 103
Morgan, Edmond 71
Morrell, Robert 23
Morris, Gouverneur 37, 48
Morris, Robert 54
Muller, Robert 10, 15, 109, 133
NAACP 93
Napoleon 27, 38
national and international copyright 64
National Assembly/Convention (France) 34, 36, 40, 59
National Emergency Civil Liberties Committee (New York) 83, 88
National Gallery of Art 105
National Lawyers Guild 85
National Park Service 107
National Portrait Gallery 73, 105
New Rochelle, New York 87

Novus Ordo Seclorum 118
nuclear weapons 23, 25, 29
obituary notice 43, 55
O'Dwyer, Paul 14, 83, 132
Open University 30
Parrington, Vernon L. 42
Paul I, Emperor of Russia 14, 66
Payson, Albert 102
Peace Studies Unit, UN Secretariat 9, 17, 19
Peale, Charles Willson 73
Pennsylvania Magazine 55, 56
Pérez de Cuéllar, Javier 9, 16, 17
Phillpot, Clive 9, 14, 70, 131, 132
Pole, J. R. 52
Polish Constitution 120
Price, Richard 34
Priestley, Joseph 34, 38
Prospects of the Rubicon 121
Quakers 41, 56, 64-66
Reagan, Ronald 12, 18, 23-25, 74
Reasons for Preserving the Life of Louis Capet 60
republicanism 13, 22, 33, 36, 39-40, 41-45, 46, 48, 52, 64, 68, 119-120
Richland, W. Bernard 88
Rights of Man 28, 35-36, 45, 48, 49, 50, 51, 58-59, 61, 67, 68, 70, 72, 84, 91, 95, 97, 106, 108, 121-122
Robbins, Caroline 51
Robespierre, Maximilian 12, 41, 122
Roland, Madame 45
Romney, George 73, 106-107
Roosevelt, Theodore 27, 42, 55, 86, 92
Rush, Benjamin 39
Russell, Bertrand 26
Scola, Ettore 72
Sharp, William 68, 73, 106
slavery 27, 55-56, 64, 75, 84-85, 96
Smiles, Samuel 73
social welfare system 51, 97
Spater, George 26
Spiegelman, Irwin 7
Spiegelman, Martha 7
Stapleton, Florence 7-8, 12, 131, 134-136

Statue of Liberty 113
Sterne, Lawrence 74
Swift, Jonathan 93, 98
Tandy, James Napper 87
Teilhard de Chardin, Pierre 7, 19
Thatcher, Margaret 74
The Age of Reason 11, 28, 37, 41-42, 45, 53, 60-61, 84, 91, 97, 108
The British Working-Class Reader 71
The English Common Reader 71
The Ragged Trousered Philanthropists 70
The Rights of Man Fiddle Tune 89
The Sons of Albion 38
Thelwell, John 52, 68
Thetford, England 75, 76, 77, 89
Thomas Jefferson Memorial Society 105
Thomas Paine Birthday Celebration 7, 92
Thomas Paine Friends 7-8
Thomas Paine Historical Society 105
Thomas Paine Hotel 109
Thomas Paine National Historical Association 7, 73, 102, 106
Thomas Paine Park 14, 88, 89
Thomas Paine Reader 26
Thomas Paine Society, UK 7, 23, 73, 91, 132
Thompson, E. P. 123-126
Thuriot, Jacques Alexis 41
Tone, Wolfe 87
Tooke, John Horne 68
Tressell, Robert 70
Trumbell, John 104
Twain, Mark 94
United Nations 7, 9, 12, 17, 19, 29, 83, 94, 96, 109, 111, 112, 113
United States Constitution 97, 111, 117, 119
United States of America 18, 22, 60, 61, 64, 97, 120
United Teilhard Trust 4, 7, 9, 12, 17, 19, 20, 23, 83, 135
Universal Declaration of Human Rights 12, 17
University for Peace 7, 17, 18, 19, 20, 22, 109, 114
Varis, Tapio 9, 18
Vaughan, Benjamin 122
Van der Weyde, William M. 102, 106
Vincent, Bernard 9, 13-14, 64, 90, 132
Visionaries of World Peace 7, 9, 17, 18, 19, 22

Voltaire (Francois-Marie Arounet) 11, 26, 74
Washington, George 27, 40, 44, 108
Wells, H. G. 28
Wesley, John 91
Whitman, Walt 92
Wilentz, Sean 9, 14-15, 89, 133
Williams, David 45
Williamson, Audrey 102
Windmill Hotel 72
Winstanley, Gerrard 93
women 56, 75
Wood, Gordon S. 119
Woodfall's Letters of Junius 101-103
Woodward, W. E. 83
Zonneveld, Leo W. 1, 7-8, 9, 16, 19, 26, 83, 130-131, 133, 134-136

Visionaries of World Peace Series

The Colloquium on Thomas Paine

'Visionaries of World Peace' embraces a series of Colloquia organized by United Teilhard Trust under the auspices of the University for Peace, aimed at honoring the world's greatest peace prophets. The series was inaugurated in 1983 with a Colloquium on the great visionary and philosopher Pierre Teilhard de Chardin.

The Colloquium on the life and work of Teilhard de Chardin and the three that followed, on Thomas Paine, Lev Nikolayevich Tolstoi, and Albert Schweitzer, were all held at United Nations Headquarters in New York, in collaboration with the Peace Studies Unit located within the UN Department of Political and Security Council Affairs.

The second in the series, the Colloquium on Thomas Paine, organized by United Teilhard Trust to celebrate the 250th Anniversary of his birth year, was held on Human Rights Day, December 10, 1987. Óscar Rafael de Jesús Arias Sánchez, President of the Republic of Costa Rica (1986-1990 and 2006-2010), where the University for Peace is headquartered, received the Nobel Prize for Peace in Stockholm, Sweden on the day of the Colloquium on Thomas Paine.

UNITED TEILHARD TRUST